AN OWNERSHIP THEORY
OF THE TRADE UNION

An Ownership Theory of the Trade Union

Donald L. Martin

University of California Press
Berkeley Los Angeles London

Published with the cooperation of the
Hoover Institution on War, Revolution and Peace

University of California Press
Berkeley and Los Angeles, California

University of California Press, Ltd.
London, England

Library of Congress Cataloging in Publication Data

Martin, Donald L.
  An ownership theory of the trade union.

  Bibliography: p. 147
  Includes index.
  1. Trade-unions. 2. Property. 3. Labor economics.
I. Title.
HD6483.M34   331.88'01   80-13147
ISBN 0-520-03884-3

Printed in the United States of America

To the memory of my father
George H. Martin
and the promise of my children
Sean and Rachel

Contents

Preface   *ix*

Acknowledgments   *x*

1. Introduction   *1*

2. A Critique of the Theoretical Literature   *6*
The Dunlop Model and Opportunity Costs   6
Politico-Economic Models   9
The Ross Model   11
The Atherton Model   16
Objectives in Conflict   23
The Wealth-Maximizing Union   27
Conclusions   30

3. An Ownership Profile of the Trade Union   *31*
Institutional Characteristics   32
Collusion Rights   32
"Suability"   33
Proprietary Interests   35
Participation Rights   36
Exhaustion of Remedies   38
Nonprofit Status   38
Structural Characteristics   39
The Structure of the Union Sector   39
Who Joins Unions?   44

4. The Basic Model in a Proprietary Paradigm   *47*
Controlling Compensatory Margins   48
Rent Production and Composition   50
Choices Affecting Utility   53
A Proprietary Paradigm   56
Wage Membership Policy   58
An Increase in Labor Demand   62

A Decrease in Demand 64
Price Level Effects on Proprietary Union Behavior 66
Heterogeneous Preferences 68
Summary 69

5. *The Nonproprietary Union* 71
The Ownership Index 73
Some General Implications 74
Changes in Demand and Union Wage-Employment-
  Membership Policy 79
A Decrease in Demand 83
Price Level Effects on Union Wage Policy 84
Ownership and the Strike Phenomenon 86
Summary 88

6. *Managerial Discretion Within the Union* 90
Managerial Constraints in a Nonproprietary Union 92
The Raid 95
Managerial Objectives 97
Union Managers and Wage-Membership Policy 102
Summary 106

7. *Price and Nonprice Rationing of Union Memberships* 108
The Proprietary Case 108
Price Discrimination in Memberships 111
The Nonproprietary Case 111
Competition for Rents by Union Leaders 115
Nonprice Rationing in a Nonproprietary Union 116
Summary 119

Notes 121

References 147

Index 153

Preface

THE history of economic thought as it pertains to economic theories of the trade union has been a disappointing one for the profession. Economists and students of industrial relations have been unable to develop a theory of the trade union which enjoys wide currency and yields testable implications concerning the formation of bargaining goals, membership policy, and relationships between union leaders and members. The models that now appear in the best-selling labor economics and industrial relations texts and in the professional journals, lack these desirable qualities.

A major source of the problem has been disagreement and confusion over just what it is unions are supposed to be maximizing, if anything. This book maintains that scholars have been unable to select an appropriate objective function for the union because they have failed to specify the set of *ownership characteristics* that permits economic theory to logically imply the union behavior they observe in the real world. The economic theory of union behavior presented here takes an entirely different approach. A theory of the trade union which clearly identifies the structure of rights faced by members and leaders to appropriate the present value of net benefits from collective action has the clear advantage of being able to reveal the relative costs to unions of pursuing different objectives or goals. For example, it will be shown that union members can be expected to behave quite differently in the formation of bargaining goals if they enjoyed private property in their membership status and could transfer their membership cards in an open market (much like shareholders in a corporation or like brokers on a stock exchange can sell their seats), than if proprietary rights in membership status were prohibited.

In the chapters that follow, union policy implications are derived under conditions where membership status is the private salable property of each member. They are then compared with implications that are derived under more realistic assumptions. The result is a richer set of testable implications that may come closer to observed union behavior than can now be found in more conventional union "models."

Although I believe the task ahead is formidable, I confess I have left the major undertakings for others. *An Ownership Theory of the Trade Union* is just that—a theory. I provide no tests of the theory in this book. Moreover, the theory addresses union objectives and not the strategy of collective bargaining, a subject that has also been difficult to treat analytically.

The idea for the "ownership theory" was born in one of those moments of revelation when the application of economic theory to what had appeared to be an unrelated problem is perceived for the first time. Studying price theory and aspects of property rights with Armen Alchian, over a decade ago, provided fertile ground for generating new ideas. Not until much later, however, did time and research support make it possible to put these ideas on paper and subject them to the criticism of colleagues. I am much indebted to the Hoover Institution for providing a year's worth of physical space, intellectual stimulation, and financial support. I am also grateful to the Law and Economics and Labor Workshops at the University of Chicago, the Labor Workshop at Washington University, the Labor Workshop at Virginia Polytechnical Institute and State University, the Law and Economics Seminar at Auburn University, and participants and sponsors of the Liberty Fund Seminar on the Economics of Nonproprietary Organizations held in Miami in 1977. These workshops and seminars led to several substantive improvements in the "ownership theory" and its implications.

Thanks are due to Yoram Barzel, Lee Benham, Tom Borcherding, Ross Eckert, H. Gregg Lewis, Walter Oi, John Pencavel, Mel Reder, Warren Sanderson, Ken Shepsle and Frederick Warren-Boulton for reading and commenting on early versions of the manuscript or parts thereof. Special thanks are extended to Armen Alchian, Ken Clarkson, Louis De Alessi, and Roger L. Miller for reading and critiquing the penultimate draft. I value them highly as colleagues and friends. Finally, I am most pleased and grateful for the constructive criticism and excellent suggestions provided by

George Hilton and George Neumann. They were most persuasive, despite my resistance to writing yet another draft, in convincing me to reorganize the book and rewrite some of the more esoteric passages.

Those persons connected with *An Ownership Theory* have made it a better work than it would have been without them. Any remaining errors, however, are my personal property.

D. L. M.

1

Introduction

THE empirical revolution that has swept the economics profession
since the Second World War has permeated almost all subdisci-
plines of the subject. The study of the economic impact of trade
unions has been a target of the new empirical techniques. Yet, unlike the study of other conventional economic institutions, such as
firms, industries, and ununionized factor markets, these empirical
efforts have proceeded without a broadly accepted economic theory
of the trade union.

The absence of an economic theory of unions is not for want of
trying. Scholars since Adam Smith (1776) have searched for an explanation of union behavior within the confines of economic
theory. Others, not so constrained, have sought explanations in
terms of political sociology (Ross 1948; Lipset, Trow, and Coleman
1956). The biggest stumbling block for economists, however, has
been the answer to the deceptively simple question asked by
Dunlop (1944) over thirty years ago: "What do unions maximize?"
Given an objective function, it is possible to derive logical implications that will serve to identify, from an otherwise bewildering
collection of facts, variables relevant to the empirical examination
of the economic impact of the trade union.

The response to Dunlop's question by economists and students
of industrial relations has been, to say the least, disappointing. The
profession has generated an embarrassing number of maximands.
It has been suggested, from time to time, that unions maximize the
wage bill,[1] the wage rate per member,[2] the utility of the membership,[3] rents generated from union monopoly power,[4] membership
size,[5] the probability of the union's survival,[6] "the economic wel-

fare of the membership,"[7] and the difference between union receipts and expenditures.[8] Some have suggested that unions are not, after all, maximizing institutions, they are satisficing institutions.[9] This cornucopia of maximands is itself evidence of the profession's failure to develop an operational model of the trade union comparable to its model of the profit maximizing firm.

One of the earliest and most obvious analogies used to describe union behavior was that of monopoly. Unions were observed to demand wage rates higher than their members could apparently achieve as individual suppliers of labor. By collectively withholding, or threatening to withhold, labor services at critical periods, wage rates could be raised to higher levels, insulated from direct competition. To all but a few observers, a union's ability to affect wage rates was evidence of monopoly power.[10] But when the *determinants* of union wage policy were sought, most modern students balked at extending the monopoly analogy to characterize union *objectives*. Although business monopolies are usually assumed to behave as if they maximize profits, it is considered naive to believe that union monopolies behave as if they maximize the labor equivalent of the present value of monopoly profits or rents—the difference between the value of the bargaining package and the membership's opportunity costs.[11]

Opposition to the wealth maximization view has been just short of unanimous (Rosen 1970; Powel 1973) and has largely focused on three fundamental objections. The first is that unions do not face discernable marginal cost functions and therefore cannot hope to discover wealth-maximizing wage policies. The second states that uncertainty about demands for union services makes information about the employment consequences of union wage demands very costly and wealth-maximizing policies very unlikely. The third holds that single valued maximands, such as the wealth maximand, ignore the multidimensional character of union objectives, the heterogeneity of member preferences, and the inherent conflict that exists between leaders and rank and file members.

But even if every one of the obstacles just enumerated were absent, economic theory might still fail to predict union behavior consistent with wealth maximization. This is so because maximands are not defined by the discernability of cost functions or the degree of certainty in the market. Profit-maximizing firms in the real world rarely enjoy the luxury of blackboard cost and revenue schedules or the certainty that academic models of the firm too often employ. Of course, a firm that operates with greater certainty about the future consequences of current actions will be better able to identify wealth-increasing opportunities than firms operating in ignorance. However, unless the firm functions under institutions that permit and facilitate the appropriation of wealth increments, wealth-maximizing behavior will not be rewarding, and economic theory clearly predicts that nonrewarding behavior will threaten the survival of the firm.

Institutional arrangements that permit residual claimants to appropriate changes in wealth are at the heart of the conventional profit-maximizing theory of the firm.[12] These arrangements constitute the structure of property rights over the use and disposition of resources. Other things the same, alterations or modifications in the structure of rights will affect the choice of maximand or objective function. This connection between property rights and choice of maximand is now well documented. Studies of ownership and decisionmaking in hospitals, insurance firms, utility companies, airlines, educational institutions, and many others reveal the close relationship between *private*-property rights in resources and the wealth maximand.[13] These private rights, to the extent that they are enforceable, permit resource owners to appropriate the capitalized value of net receipt streams, making wealth-maximizing resource use too costly to forsake, relative to other objectives. Conversely, hypotheses that employ nonwealth maximands have been found to yield relatively better predictions about organizational behavior, where private-property rights are absent or substantially attenuated; as, for example, in government agencies, labor managed firms, and mutual savings and loan associations.[14]

These findings suggest that knowledge of the ownership structure of an organization is a necessary step in identifying the appropriate maximand or objective function for any given organization. Unfortunately, students of union activity have ignored the economic implications that arise from the structure of property rights found in unions. As a result, maximands for models of union behavior have been chosen ad hoc. For example, John Dunlop's widely cited *wage bill* objective (the product of the union negotiated wage rate and the employed membership) ignores the majority rule institution in most unions and the voting rights exercised by their members. These institutional constraints are inconsistent with the choice of a wage bill maximand, as the literature critique in the next chapter demonstrates. Analogously, Arthur Ross and, more recently, Wallace Atherton devote considerable attention to "organizational survival"[15] as a union objective, yet neither specified the incentive mechanism (and in particular the set of constraints) that would cause leaders to take account of the future survival consequences of their current decisions. Without this important link between the structure of rights facing members and leaders and union behavior, the door is open to the adoption of almost any would-be maximand.

With little theoretical guidance, different scholars, as we noted, have selected different union maximands. Moreover, as more and more scholars have attempted to answer the question "what do unions maximize?" more and more maximands have appeared. This has led at least one recent, and despairing, observer to conclude that " . . . the problem of modeling trade union behavior has proved to be virtually intractable."[16] This prognosis is surely too dismal, especially in light of the fact that no systematic examination of the ownership characteristics of unions has been incorporated into the modeling of union objectives.

If there is to be a tractable and refutable theory of the trade union, that is consistent with the rest of economic theory, it must be founded on an explicit structure of property rights that identifies both costs and rewards faced by members and their leaders. Some rights structures will be consistent with the choice of a wealth maximand for the union, while others will not. Knowledge of the actual ownership structure in unions will therefore aid in the derivation of implications about union behavior that have a greater chance of being coincident with the evidence bearing on that behavior.

In the chapters that follow, this book develops two different models of the trade union. One is based on proprietary assumptions, i.e., private-property rights, for members, in the capital value of rents arising from union activity. The other model is based on nonproprietary assumptions. That is, an alternative model of union behavior is derived from economic theory, where members are prohibited from appropriating a pro-rated share of the capital value of future union rents. It will be shown that the implications derived from these models, concerning wage, benefit, membership and employment policies, are markedly different, and that the institutional arrangements that actually characterize the ownership structure of unions do not favor selection of a wealth maximand for an organizational objective.

Before we discuss these ownership models it will be useful to review and critique some of the more widely referenced theories of union behavior. In this context, chapter two will critically examine the three historical objections to the use of the wealth maximand for unions, mentioned above, and the alternative models they inspired. Following this, chapter two briefly examines a relatively recent attempt at modeling a wealth-maximizing union, exposing the sensitivity of its implications to implicit assumptions about the structure of property rights in unions.

In chapter three we examine the nature of existing legal and voluntary institutions that define the opportunity set within which union members and union leaders conduct their affairs. A brief but informative membership profile of unionism in the United States is also presented. Chapter four offers a model of union behavior that assumes union members enjoy private-property rights in the capital value of future union rents and personal claims to the net revenues collected by the union. Several implications relevant to union wage, benefit, employment and membership policies are derived. Chapter five relaxes the proprietary assumptions of the previous chapter and generates a number of competing implications from a nonproprietary model based on the constraints discussed in chapter three. Chapter six introduces the union manager as a separate functionary and discusses several implications concerning his behavior and its influence on the union's policy goals derived in chapters four and five. A prominent feature of this chapter is the discussion of union managerial discretion where monitoring costs are positive, and unions are characterized by the institutional constraints outlined in chapter three. Finally, chapter seven treats the question of price and nonprice rationing of union membership under proprietary and nonproprietary assumptions. The well-known practices of "underpricing" union memberships and the use of nonprice rationing are explained in terms of the nonproprietary models of chapters five and six.

2

A Critique of the
Theoretical Literature

In CHAPTER one we noted that aversion to the wealth maximand, a characteristic of the conventional theoretical literature on unions, is the result of three widely embraced objections to the union-firm analogy. The purpose of this chapter is to review and critique both the objections and the alternative theories of union behavior that they inspired. It will be shown in this and succeeding chapters, that the failure of previous writers to subject the ownership characteristics of trade unions to economic analysis is, in large part, responsible for their failure to develop operational theories of the trade union that are consistent with the rest of economic theory.

The first objection, and by far the more universal, rests upon the observation that unions do not purchase and resell labor services, in the same way that business firms purchase and resell nonhuman resources. As a result, these critics argue that the membership's marginal supply prices (that reflect their preferences for leisure and their opportunities in alternative employments) do not enter as marginal costs in the decision calculus of the union.[1] In the absence of information regarding relevant opportunity costs, the union is not equipped to maximize collective rents for the membership and it is therefore unlikely to do so.[2]

THE DUNLOP MODEL AND OPPORTUNITY COSTS

Far and away the best known economic model of the trade union, that seeks to remedy the alleged opportunity cost deficiency, is John Dunlop's wage bill maximization hypothesis. Although his search for a maximand generated several alternative models of union wage policy, including one claiming to maximize collective rents (i.e., wealth), he concluded that "the most suitable generalized model of the trade union for analytical purposes is probably that which depicts the maximization of the wage bill[3] for the total membership."[4]

Dunlop's innovation was to substitute a union membership function for the marginal cost function, where the former is defined as "an (upward sloping) array of minimum affiliation offers as viewed from the trade union (leaders)."[5] This function is operative as a constraint where it intersects the conventional downward sloping labor demand schedule at rates (*minimum affiliation offers*) equal to or greater than unit elasticity. Unit elasticity, of course, is where total wage income is at a maximum. Maximum total *wage income* is the product of the collective wage rate and employment. This may be equal to or greater than the *wage bill,* which is a function of *employed members.* Uniform wage rates below unit elasticity or, more generally, below the intersection of demand and membership curves, by definition, will not increase the gross income of the membership. Unless some pooling arrangement is made with the new employees, lower rates will transfer income away from existing members.

So long as the number of would-be union affiliates, at the maximizing wage rate, does not exceed the quantity of labor demanded at that rate, it may be concluded that all members will find employment.[6] Maximizing the wage bill at the point of unit elasticity or alternatively at a point where demand and membership curves intersect, will therefore yield employment for more than a majority of the membership. This has raised an important objection to the wage bill maximand. The union (or its leaders) does (do) not look to *all* members for political support, only to the majority of them. Given its political constraints (i.e., majority rule), why would a union necessarily set the wage goal at either of the above two points on the labor demand curve? An even higher wage rate, for example, could generate a wage bill for a majority of members in excess of the share they would otherwise receive.[7] Thus, the location of Dunlop's membership function, relative to unit elasticity, cannot identify the majority wage rate nor membership-employment unambiguously.

Such criticism, however, ignores the possibility that minority interests may find it worthwhile to compensate the majority for adopting a wage policy more favorable to the former. This possibility was recognized by Atherton (1973), but mistakenly used as a counterargument supporting the Dunlop wage bill thesis.[8] According to Atherton, "There will always be an incentive for some members to pay others to vote for the wage [rate] at which total wage income [wage bill] would be maximized. With a free market in votes, the membership would arrive at [for them] the Pareto-optimal income maximizing wage after all."[9] In this manner 51 percent of the membership is made just as well off as they would have been had the wage rate been higher.[10]

Of particular interest, this argument acknowledges that "the execution of such compensatory arrangements would require . . . that those who pay for their jobs end up with *net income* larger than they could achieve in alternative employments."[11] Atherton's explicit recognition, however, that the membership's opportunity costs are crucial to wage bill maximization, reduces that hypothesis to question-begging. That is, if income from alternative employments is important to those who must pay compensation (to retain their jobs) and if this consideration, according to Atherton, influences the determination of the maximand, why wouldn't income from alternative employments be important to those who *receive* the compensation, that is, the majority of members, and why wouldn't this consideration influence the determination of the maximand also? But this implies that opportunity costs enter the union's maximization process, however indirectly, and this implication explicitly conflicts with Dunlop's reason for introducing the membership function and assuming a wage bill maximand in the first place; that is, an absence of a membership opportunity cost function facing the union.

It is rather ironic that Atherton's defense of the Dunlop wage bill maximand must acknowledge the existence of something that the latter claimed was absent from the union's calculus. This seeming paradox results from a failure to focus directly on the relevant problem in modeling unions. Dunlop chose a nonrent maximand for his model of a union *because* he believed unions do not sell the labor services of their members *as if* these organizations *owned* them. Dunlop's observation acknowledges, in effect, that unions do not have private-property rights in members or in their labor services, as do firms selling nonlabor resources. Unions, therefore, cannot be expected to pursue the same type of objective function as firms. It is a long leap, however, between the ownership *defect* just mentioned and Dunlop's specific choice of a wage bill maximand. On the other hand, implicit in Atherton's defense of Dunlop's maximand is the observation that members, if not the union, do *own* their labor services and therefore have a notion of their opportunity costs. Moreover, members possess voting rights that may be traded internally for a quid pro quo.[12] These two elements in the structure of members' rights, however, are consistent with a rent maximand for the union and not a wage bill maximand, especially in the one period models discussed by Dunlop. As long as *all* rents occur in the present, and transaction costs are not prohibitive, members will be better off if the median voter chooses the wage policy that maximizes rents. Once the single period assumption is relaxed, however, and neither the union nor its members possess private property rights in the capital value of future monopoly rent streams, rent, in present value terms, is also an inappropriate maximand for a model of union behavior.[13]

In the final analysis, perhaps the most telling criticism that can be leveled against the wage bill hypothesis, aside from questions of logical structure, is the obvious paucity of testable implications. Earlier critics, such as Reder (1952) were quick to point out that testable implications depended upon specification of the relevant membership function.[14] Specification for different subgroups implies different wage bill policies. Since the theory offers no guidance in identifying "the" membership function relevant to a particular union or situation, unambiguous predictions are not forthcoming.[15]

POLITICO-ECONOMIC MODELS

The origins of the modern revolt against purely economic interpretations of union behavior (i.e., against models with single valued wealth or income maximands) may be found in Arthur Ross's seminal work, *Trade Union Wage Policy*. This work is perhaps best known for the controversy it created over union perceptions of the wage-employment relationship,[16] the basis of the second objection to the wealth maximand, and its criticism of union models fashioned too closely after profit-maximizing theories of the firm. Although few students of the trade union are unfamiliar with Ross's description of union behavior as "political" rather than "economic," only a few have been able to deduce operational hypotheses from his propositions.[17] However, in the substance of Ross's description of union objectives there is a perceptive outline or framework for a model of union behavior, which I call the Ross "model," that will be discussed below. Before examining the Ross "model," his skepticism of the wage-employment function, as a clearly perceived relationship within union management, is examined and challenged.

This second objection to extending the wealth maximization hypothesis to trade unions asserts that even if unions desire to maximize collective rents, unforeseen shifts in product and factor demands make the future employment consequences of current wage demands and the current consequences of past wage agreements virtually impossible to interpret. Consequently, unions would be insensitive to the employment effects of their wage demands[18] (Ross 1948, p. 80; Lindblom 1949, chap. 6). At the time, this objection created a great deal of controversy. Together with the implications associated with the claim that unions are unconstrained by opportunity cost, it has been used (never without serious challenge) to move the determination of union bargaining goals outside the bounds of economic analysis (Ross 1948; Kerr 1948).

Like its contemporary, the controversy over "marginalism" in the theory of the firm (Lester 1946; Machlup 1946), the rejection of a labor demand curve in the decision calculus of unions is an incorrect inference from the recognition that information is not costless. From the existence of uncertainty it is deduced (erroneously) that both firms and unions will not make wealth-maximizing decisions.

If we accept the notion that a union's perception of the wage-employment relationship is shrouded in conjecture, and therefore rendered nonoperational, it is then difficult to explain its characteristic hypersensitivity to the "cheap labor threat" associated with lower-priced foreign goods, multinational corporations, immigration, right-to-work laws, and the repeal of child labor and minimum wage statutes. It is well known that unions, operating where product demands are relatively inelastic (and, ceteris paribus, therefore inelastic labor demands), seem to "do better" (Weiss 1969; Lewis 1963). That is, they increase the wealth of their members relatively more than in industries where product demand is more elastic. It is doubtful that this observation escapes the unions themselves. Union efforts to establish cartels among employers in coal, clothing, trucking, construction and textiles were not merely to improve extractable rents in these industries. Cartels reduce the price elasticity of final product demands and, other things the same, the elasticity of factor demands as well.

Efforts to differentiate final products produced in union shops by the use of union labeling (Bird and Robinson 1972) or to otherwise encourage the boycott of nonunion products, have their anticipated reward in making demands for labor less wage elastic. Promotion of tariff protection has the same effect (Mitchell 1970). Work rules, tying minimum crews to capital equipment, reduce the elasticity of demand for labor by reducing the elasticity of substitution among inputs (Hartman 1969). Promotion of legislation or contracts prohibiting females or minors from performing certain classes of work reduces the elasticity of labor demand by reducing the supply elasticity of complementary factors (Petshek 1950; Hilton 1959). All these efforts on the part of unions to shape the labor market environment to their favor and make it more comprehensible require the expenditure of resources. This resource commitment reflects the perception that unions have of the employment effects of monopoly wage rates, and suggests the potential usefulness of *economic* analysis for explaining trade union behavior.

THE ROSS MODEL

Ross views the union as the product of three interdependent goals which he identifies as: maximum economic welfare for rank and file members, the union's *formal* purpose; the survival and growth of the organization, its *institutional* objective; and the exercise of *personal* power by the union's leadership as an expression of the personal survival goals of union management.

The formal purpose or rationale of the organization is to maximize the "economic welfare" of the membership. Economic welfare is a function of wages, hours, working conditions, economic security, protection against managerial abuse, and "union rights of self-determination" (Ross, p. 27). Critics since Ross have interpreted this goal to suggest that a wealth maximand would be inconsistent with many of the elements that define economic welfare for rank and filers. This constitutes the first of three parts that identify the third objection to the use of a wealth maximand, as presented in chapter one. But surely "nonpecuniary" objectives per se are not inconsistent with wealth maximization. Demands for licensing, regulation, quality control, and health and safety standards by businesses in the product markets have rarely been seen as evidence rejecting the profit maximizing model.

Many "nonpecuniary" objectives promoted by firms have the effect of improving their wealth positions and may be treated as investments. Likewise, work rules may be interpreted as devices for insulating the union's monopoly position and the wealth of the membership from the competition of capital and labor substitutes. Work sharing, overtime penalties, and supplemental unemployment benefits may contribute to the pooling of monopoly rents among the membership. Grievance and arbitration procedures, so closely associated with the nonpecuniary interests of unions, have their counterparts in the arbitration of contract disputes among firms in the output market. The latter reality, however, appears not to threaten the relevance of profit-maximization in the theory of the firm. Why should it threaten the relevance of rent-maximization in a theory of the union?

The *institutional* goal is defined as survival and growth of the organization. Union leadership is surrounded by conflicts of interest, emanating from and within the rank and file, the employers, other unions, and government. Somehow it must accommodate these diverse interests. "It is at this point that the formal purpose of the organization is supplanted by more vital forces—the instinct for survival and the impulse toward growth." Although, according to Ross, the coincidence of formal purpose and institutional objective may be quite common (for reasons he does not divulge), he also asserts that "a healthy institution will look to its own necessities" should a conflict in objectives arise (Ross, p. 26).

Ross was specific in his description of some of the more important kinds of interest conflicts that could threaten a union's survival.

> The wage income of the union membership may account for widely different proportions of total cost in their respective industries. Even within a single industry there are employees of profitable and unprofitable firms, and the employees residing in high wage and low wage areas. Moreover, there are young and old workers, fast

and slow workers, male and female workers, . . . employed and unemployed. Nonhomogeneity of membership gives rise to conflicts of interest, it is one of the most delicate *political* tasks of union leadership to reconcile these conflicts in formulating a wage program. [Ross, 1948, pp. 31-32, italics supplied]

These political tasks, according to Ross, are important features that militate against a merely conventional economic interpretation of union behavior, and it is this view that represents the second part of the third objection to wealth maximization.

In and of themselves, however, "differing interests" are insufficient, a priori, to reject the wealth maximand as a likely candidate for interpreting the behavior of firms or unions. Rather, we should concentrate on the costs of accommodating divergent interests and the observable forms that accommodation might take. Yet, neither Ross nor his contemporaries explain why the costs of reconciling differences among members in a wealth-maximizing union might be higher than the costs of reconciling differences among members in the essentially *noneconomic* or *political* model of union behavior suggested in his *Trade Union Wage Policy*.

The third objective that Ross identifies in the union concerns the personal ambitions of the leaders. "In the failure of voluntary identification [with the institutional and formal objectives of the union] and in the absence of social controls requiring compulsory identification, the leaders are governed by their own survival needs and their own ambitions, which are at variance with those of the organization."[19] This is the last part of the third objection to the use of a wealth maximand (Ross, p. 26).

However, identity of interests between owners and managers are neither necessary nor sufficient conditions for profit maximization in the theory of the firm, ceteris paribus. If the costs of detecting and policing deviations from profit maximization are zero or "not prohibitive," if exit, entry, and take-over are not impeded, and if there exists an efficient market for managers, the importance of differences in objectives can be relegated to "the second order of smalls" and no modifications in the profit-maximizing theory of the firm are warranted.[20] It is not uncommon for union leaders, dues hikes, strikes, and decertification to be subject to the popular vote of the membership. Members often have recourse to the N.L.R.B. and the courts under conditions where union leadership is arbitrary and unlawful. "Raiding" by rival unions has not been an uncommon practice. In other words, it is not as if the exercise of managerial discretion in unions were totally unfettered (McConnell 1954). Without first examining the institutional and market constraints facing union leaders in the pursuit of their separate interests, an out-of-hand rejection of the single valued wealth maximand would seem premature.[21]

Ross, most perceptively, suggests that the three kinds of union objectives, *formal*, *institutional*, and *personal*, may analogously describe the conflicting objectives of almost any institution, be it business, church or state (Ross, pp. 22-23). That is, almost every institution has *some* formal objective or stated purpose, which can exist independently of the organization itself, while its officials may pursue an institutional objective, that is, institutional survival, as well as personal ambition.

Ross has no problem rejecting any analogy between unions and firms. "Although comparable with a business firm in some respects, it is so dissimilar in other respects that the analogy is of questionable value" (Ross, p. 43). What is remarkable about this assertion is that it does not rest on a discovery that the two institutions fail to share a common objective, that is, a single valued pecuniary maximand. Rather, Ross suggests that business firms are more likely to exhibit behavior consistent with their *formal* purpose or rationale than are unions, and that this is why the latter should be treated as *political* rather than as *economic* institutions. This conclusion, according to Ross, is based on dissimilarities in the *constraints* faced by the respective managements of these institutions. Deviations from formal objectives are relatively costly for union members to detect, when compared with the costs facing stockholders, because "corporate managers must operate under the surveillance of cost accountants and financial officers who have the function of steering leadership activities toward the . . . formal purpose of the enterprise. Corresponding agencies of a rudimentary form are sometimes found in a union organization but they are probably less of a drag upon the leadership . . . because the formal purpose of the union is less capable of measurement" (Ross, p. 27). This distinction suggests a fundamental difference in the costs of information to the "rank and file" in the respective institutions. To Ross, "economic welfare" is composed of phenomena of incommensurate dimension while profit need be measured in only one dimension (Ross, p. 44).[22]

To the extent that union leaders derive some rewards from the size of membership, their incentives to raise the price of labor, where labor is not fully organized, may differ from the incentives of managers of business firms, with comparable monopoly power, to raise the prices of their products (Ross, p. 28). Although Ross offers no comment, this suggests another reason for a divergence in the pursuit of the formal objectives of the respective organizations. Because employers are often hostile to unions and union leaders, threatening their survival, the costs to leaders of pursuing formal objectives are higher than otherwise, and leaders respond by sacrificing these objectives for institutional ones. Moreover, to survive as a leader or union manager at the local level often requires holding the allegiance of a heterogeneous membership, in contrast to the relatively less complicated task for the corporate official of cultivating and maintaining the approval of a relatively few corporate executives above him. Tenure at the local level is very uncertain. "In consequence it is more difficult for the local union official to achieve complete identification with the institution" (Ross, p. 30). At the national level, however, union officers are recognized for their "reasonableness" and "responsibility" relative to local officers. Ross attributes this not to their maturity or experience but rather "the most important reason is that they are better *insulated from rank and file pressure*" (Ross, p. 31, italics supplied). This suggests that more certain tenure, *when obtained by insulation* from rank and file pressure, also has the effect of encouraging deviations from the formal objectives of the union (albeit, perhaps, of a different kind).

We may sum up by observing that the distinction between the trade union and the firm that caused Ross to refer to the union as a political rather than an economic institution and to strongly reject any analogy between unions and product market monopolies, was not the difference in formal maximands, but rather the difference in constraints facing decision makers in the respective organizations. Unfortunately, Ross focused on only manifestations of these differences, such as were found in cost accounting practices and in other financial management practices of unions, and neglected their source. The absence of a proprietary interest in the present value of union monopoly rents lowers the cost to members of ignoring sound financial management practices in unions and suggests an explanation for the differences Ross observed. In the chapters that follow, we will argue that dissimilarities in behavioral constraints between firms and unions are a function of dissimilarities in the ownership structures of these organizations.

When Ross attempted an alternative explanation of union wage policy, within and across unionized firms and industries, he offered no testable propositions, per se. We are told that the observed pattern of wages results from political pressures of members, employers, rival unions, and unorganized labor that are characterized by "equitable comparisons" and circumscribed by "orbits of coercive comparisons," concepts that Ross and others failed to make operational (Ross, chap. 3).[23]

Recently, some economists (Atherton 1973; Ashenfelter and Johnson 1969) have attempted to model, in a more rigorous fashion, certain propositions about union behavior that have their origin in Ross's work just described. Their common theoretical ground appears to be located in the behavioral implications associated with a separation of interests between members and leaders, i.e., the dichotomy between the union's formal purpose and the survival and growth objectives of the leadership.

In his book *Theory of Union Bargaining Goals* (1973), Wallace Atherton explicitly adopts Ross's trichotomy of interests within the union for the purposes of constructing a model capable of explaining and predicting the objectives but not the outcomes of union bargaining. The latter requires a theory of bargaining between employer and union that reflects mutually preferable outcomes. This is attempted with some success by Ashenfelter and Johnson, who also adopt a distinction between members and leaders in the spirit of Ross. However, their analysis focuses, as it should, on the interests of employers as well. More will be said about the Ashenfelter–Johnson model in a later chapter. At this point it is more important to focus on Atherton's work. To my knowledge this will be the first time the Atherton model has been subject to a substantive critique.[24]

THE ATHERTON MODEL

Atherton's work is more than just a rigorous restatement of Ross's view of union behavior. It is an impressive attempt to synthesize the "political" and "economic" aspects of union behavior that have been the subject of debate these past thirty years. To this end and in sharp contrast to Ross, the elements in Atherton's maximands for members and leaders are subject to a wage-employment constraint perceivable and decipherable by the leadership.

Atherton hypothesizes that the formal purpose of the union is to maximize the utility of members.[25] Utility for a given member is a function of leisure (j), the number of employed members (e), the length of strikes in days (S), and disposable real pecuniary income (y), where $Y = wh\text{-}t/p$, and w is a money wage rate, h is hours worked per week, t is an income tax, and p is the price level. In Atherton's notation:

Maximize $U = U(wh\text{-}t/p, j, e, S)$ (2.1)

subject to an employment or labor demand constraint

$e = e(w,h)$ (2.1a)

and to a strike constraint reflecting the employer's willingness to sustain a strike in terms of days

$S = S(w,h).$ (2.1b)

Except for S, the utility-affecting elements in (2.1) may be divided into bargainable and nonbargainable variables. The former are restricted to the money wage rate and to the length of the work week in hours. The latter (t, p, and e) are either beyond the direct control of the union or usually not included in negotiations. However, to the extent that unions affect wage rates, they indirectly affect employment.[26] The strike variable affects utility by interrupting the daily flow of income. Analogous to the symmetry between the disutility of work and the utility of leisure, the disutility of strike days may be more easily understood if redefined as the utility of *income earning days*. Individual members are willing to trade off some number of days they would otherwise be earning income, at the current wage rate, for an increment in the wage rate that might result from the withholding of their services, other things the same.[27]

Given perfect certainty, identical preferences, the employer's labor demand and strike curves, (as expressed in 2.1a and 2.1b respectively) and holding t, p, and h constant, Atherton derives the union's utility maximizing bargaining goal, geometrically.[28] Figures 2.1 and 2.2 describe this result in wage-employment space and wage-strike space respectively. In figure 2.1, the ordinate axis measures alternative levels of real income by alternative wage rates, since t, p, and h are held constant. The abscissa measures the number of workers employed.[29] Each z curve represents alternative

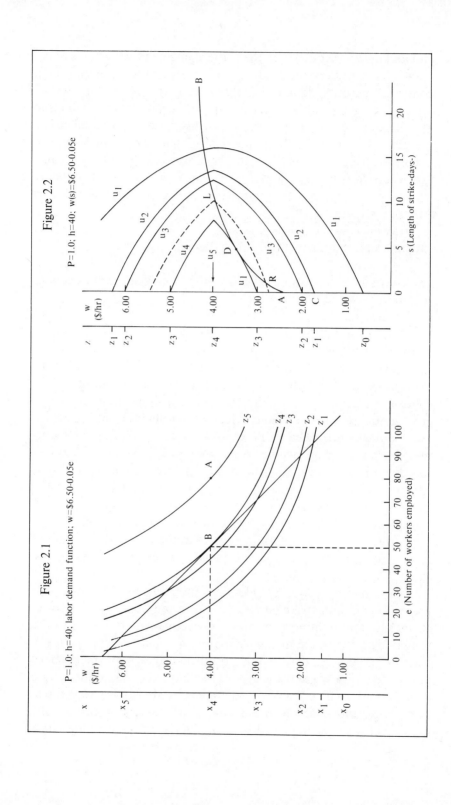

Figure 2.1

P=1.0; h=40; labor demand function; w=$6.50-0.05e

Figure 2.2

P=1.0; h=40; w(s)=$6.50-0.05e

combinations of real income, as measured by (w), and employment (e) yielding the same level of utility to all members.[30] The preference direction is northeast, meaning higher wage rates (real income) and more employment are preferred to less of both. The employer's labor demand curve (DD) is superimposed on the preference map and identifies combinations of (w) and (e) that are achievable for the union from those that are not. However, the optimal wage-employment goal for the union can be identified in figure 2.1 only if employers agree not to resist union wage demands by sustaining strikes. Under these conditions, point (B) represents the wage rate above which the union will not push its demands for fear that the consequent fall in employment will place members on a lower level of utility. Likewise wage rates below (B) are also nonoptimal because the fall in income to existing members will lower utility. Point (B) is called the "no-strike-optimum." Once we admit the possibility that employers are willing to sustain strikes of some positive duration before giving into wage demands, the two-dimensional analysis must shift to wage-strike length space, defined in figure 2.2.

Atherton assumes that unions trade off income earning days for higher wage rates, so that over the relevant range, indifference curves *in wage-strike length space* are positively sloped. However, since shorter strikes are preferred to longer strikes at the same wage rate, the preference direction is toward the ordinate axis. These properties may be observed in figure 2.2, where strike length is measured on the abscissa and wage-rates on the ordinate axis. The unusual shape of the indifference curves derives from the relationship between the preference function and the demand curve in figure 2.1. In that diagram, it should be noted, the demand curve cuts every z curve, below z_4, at two different wage rates. Thus, all wage rates above and below $4.00 are on lower levels of z. This may be shown in figure 2.2 by superimposing, on the ordinate axis and to the left of the wage rates, the levels of z cut by the demand curve in the wage-employment space of figure 2.1.

The wage rates on the ordinate axis in figure 2.2 correspond to the levels of utility (z_i) touched by the demand curve in figure 2.1. For example, wage rates at $6.00 and 2.00 are on z_2 and correspond to U_3 in 2.2 at *zero strike days*. As before, z_4 is the no-strike optimum at $4.00 and corresponds to U_5 *at zero strike days*. Since longer strikes produces disutility at a given wage rate, this should be reflected in the shapes of the indifference curves in figure 2.2. Given a set of wage rates that are associated with a given level of utility (U_i) at zero strike days, those wage rates must be associated with even lower levels of utility as strike days are increased.[31] Moreover, for any positive number of strike days, utility is lowered as wage rates diverge, in either direction, from the $4.00 optimum.

Superimposed in the wage-strike space of figure 2.2 is the employer's strike function, AS. Utility is maximized for the union at the *membership optimum*, where the rate at which it is willing to sacrifice income earning days for wage rate increments is equal to the rate at which the employer is willing to sustain losses, in terms of strike days, to avoid paying out a wage increment. Any wage demand greater or less than at (D), such as the no-strike optimum $4.00, is associated with a strike length that is suboptimal. This is so because the maximum level of utility achievable at given AS, is at L a utility level less than U_4. Moreover, the wage rate defined at (D) also defines the level of employment that maximizes the membership's utility, in wage-employment space (figure 2.1), *given the strike constraint.* It should not be overlooked, however, that the Atherton model assumes rather than derives the strike behavior of the union. That is, we are not given a model of the bargaining strike decision by the union. The employer's strike-length function merely tells us the length of time an employer will resist a strike before giving in. It does not tell us the conditions under which the union will call a strike. This then is Atherton's basic model, or model 1 as he calls it.[32]

However, the model becomes ambiguous as soon as comparative statics are attempted. If, other things the same, price level changes affect the membership's real income disproportionately when compared with their employer,[33] or where a tax rise lowers members' relative real income, Atherton's model does not yield unambiguous predictions concerning the new wage strike-length objective desired by the union (Atherton, p. 60). Variations in h similarly fail to yield unambiguous implications. In an attempt to remedy these problems, Atherton introduces his concept of a *target zone:* " . . . there may be one or more wage rates, weekly real income levels, levels of employment, etc. for the getting or keeping of which the union or its members will give up a *great deal* (of employment, leisure, strike time, etc.)" (Atherton, p. 61, italics supplied).

Within this zone, in two-dimensional wage-strike length space, the rate at which the union is willing to trade off the relevant utility affecting elements is *significantly* different from the marginal rates of substitution outside the zone. According to Atherton, "Our concept of the target zone is similar to that underlying the near-kinks in Cartter's (1959) union indifference maps" (Atherton, p. 70). Given some predetermined target wage and holding the labor demand and strike functions constant, a rise in any one of the parameters p, t, or h has the effect of shifting up and *flattening out the indifference map*, in figures 2.1 and 2.2, above the initial target rate. By specifying the signs of changes in marginal rates of substitution between utility affecting variables as parameters are altered, Atherton attempts to resolve the ambiguities that plagued his less restricted model.[34]

Despite his claim that the target zone provides a "theoretical basis" for making statements about the real world,[35] its introduction, like the introduction of Cartter's kinked utility function for trade unions two decades ago, is a deus ex machina that severely limits the general applicability of the Atherton model. Conspicuously absent from his analysis is an apparatus for determining the *target rate* that is the lower bound of the target zone, and therefore for determining the target zone itself; "Just why this is a target rate is not specified" (Atherton, p. 64). Clearly, this must mean that the target zone is ad hoc. Without a mechanism for determining the target rate, testable comparative static predictions are impossible and the target zone and the model itself are of little use in answering the kinds of questions Atherton has put to it.[36] But this should not be construed to suggest that Atherton's utility maximization apparatus for rank and file members is useless in answering other questions about union behavior. Before turning to these questions, it will be instructive to compare the results from Dunlop's wage bill maximizing model and Atherton's utility maximizing model (as presented in fig. 2.1) with the monopoly rent maximizing solution.

Figure 2.3 presents a simple rent-maximization model where the wage rate is the only variable over which the union has any *direct* influence. In wage-employment space (quadrant A), SS is the labor supply curve (for convenience identical to the union's marginal cost curve), DD is the labor demand curve, and MR is the union's marginal revenue curve. Rents are maximized at the employment-wage coordinates ($\bar{w}$, $\bar{e}$), where SS = MR. This result

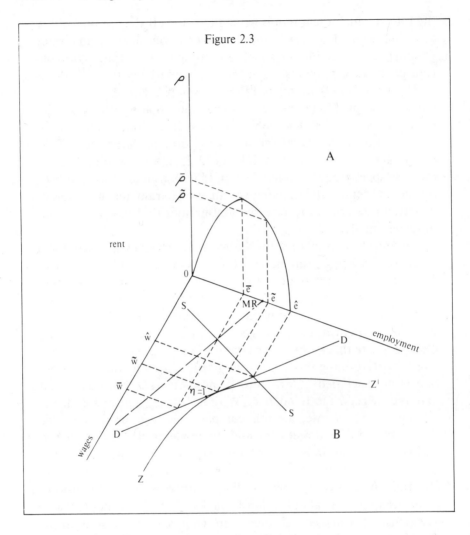

Figure 2.3

maps into rent-employment space (quadrant B) at the rent-employment coordinates (ϱ, $\bar{e}$), where the rent curve reaches a maximum. Note that at the market clearing wage rate and employment coordinates ($\hat{w}$, $\hat{e}$), rents are zero. Now let us consider Dunlop's wage bill model. Unless the intersection of his membership function (not shown) and the DD curve happens to occur at the ($\bar{w}$, $\bar{e}$) coordinates, where $\varrho = \bar{\varrho}$, Dunlop's wage bill model will yield results which do not maximize rents. However, as we have shown earlier, the Dunlop solution is unstable and there will be pressure, from at least some union members, to move toward $\bar{\varrho}$ or ($\bar{w}$, $\bar{e}$). Next consider the Atherton model. Unless the utility maximizing solution (a tangency of DD and an indifference curve in wage rate-employment space, e.g., ZZ' in fig. 2.3) occurs at the ($\bar{w}$, $\bar{e}$) coordinates, Atherton's "no strike optimum" solution (shown here at coordinates w, e) will not maximize rents,[37] at least where preferences are identical.[38] However, if preferences are not identical, so that for some subset of members' utility is maximized at $\bar{\varrho}$, there will be some amount of wealth that the members of this set will be willing to transfer to other members, which will persuade the latter to vote for rent-maximizing policies and yet be no worse off for it. This suggests that, other things the same, Atherton's basic utility maximization model and the simple rent-maximization model outlined above are capable of yielding identical results under reasonable conditions.[39]

OBJECTIVES IN CONFLICT

As mentioned earlier, Atherton's contribution to trade union theory focuses on the trichotomy of interests between the rank and file and the leadership, and within the rank and file itself. Where the *formal* purpose of the union is to maximize the utility of rank and file members, the union's *institutional* objective is identified with the leadership. Atherton joins Ross in listing the survival of the union as a bargaining agent and the political survival of its leaders under the rubric of *institutional goals.*[40] However, as it turns out, in his model 2, Atherton adopts Berkowitz's (1954) *net revenue* maximand for the union's insitutional objective and incorporates the above two goals as *constraints* on the leadership's objective function (Atherton, p. 73). Net revenue is a function of dues receipts and the costs of union services and activities generally provided to the membership.[41] Curiously, there is much discussion by Atherton of the effects of wage policy on the future survival of the union, yet he never suggests that the revenue maximand should be expressed in present value terms (Atherton, chap. 4, esp. pp. 87 and 96). More importantly, discussion of the institutional arrangements that would cause leaders and members to give sufficient weight to the future survival of the union is wholly absent.

In the simplest case it is assumed that members do not ratify wage agreements, dues are independent of wage rates, and a union shop clause obtains. Since strikes and less employment lower net revenues, the leadership will seek a wage policy that increases employment and decreases the probability of strikes, ceteris paribus.[42] However, for the rank and file there is some minimal level of satisfaction (from wages, hours, numbers employed, and income-earning days employed) below which a critical fraction of members will threaten the survival of the union as their bargaining representative, or the political survival of the incumbent officials.[43] The wage rate-employment-strike length policy that maximizes net dues revenues, *subject to the political survival constraints* just discussed, and to an economic survival constraint requiring all costs to be covered by dues receipts, is defined as the institutional *optimum*. This optimum yields wage rates and strike lengths equal to or less than the wages and strike days associated with the membership optimum, defined above,[44] but still greater than the wage rate associated with the market-clearing magnitude (Atherton, p. 75).

Choice of a net revenue maximand for the leadership appears paradoxical in the Atherton model.[45] On the one hand, members are assumed to maximize a multivalued utility function. On the other hand, leaders are assumed to maximize a single valued net receipts function. Why the apparent difference? An answer is hinted at by Atherton when he states:

> Unions and their leaders typically have objectives beyond the retention of current bargaining rights and their accomplishment usually requires money. This applies to organizing drives or the provision of new services to members, just as it does to the enjoyment of leadership conferences in Honolulu or Miami Beach. [Atherton, p. 73]

This statement may be interpreted to mean that net revenue maximization is a proxy for a utility maximand, in that activities beyond those designed to secure tenure for the leadership have utility affecting payoffs in both pecuniary (salary increases)[46] and nonpecuniary (e.g., trips to Miami Beach) form. The more income generated over and above the costs of servicing member demands, at given dues-prices, the more that is available to satisfy the particular tastes of the leadership. This proposition leads Atherton to the hypothesis that leaders will attempt to maximize net revenues. That is, there is no actual difference in objectives. For union leaders revenue maximization and utility maximization are identical. The intended analogy to the behavior of the private-for-profit firm is clear[47] and is even made explicit in Berkowitz (1954), whose model Atherton has adopted. To the extent that utility enhancing elements consumed inside and outside the firm cost money, it is always in the firm's interest to maximize residual receipts, since the larger the residual the more of all goods available to the owners(s).

Whether the purchase of a rug is for the home or office, the greater the profits, the more valuable the rug that can be purchased.[48] This implication is based on five auxiliary assumptions: (a) the firm or entrepreneur has private, enforceable property rights in the residual difference between revenues and costs; (b) the rights to residual claims are transferable; (c) there is a market in nonowner managerial skills; (d) transactions costs are not prohibitive; and (e) the utility derivable from any good may be acquired outside the firm.

All but the last of these assumptions represent constraints in the profit-maximizing theory of the firm. More importantly, they are constraints on the firm's decision maker-owner. Change one or more, and the logical implications that derive from the entrepreneur as utility maximizer will differ from those that derive from the conventional theory of the profit-maximizing firm. This is because the profit-maximization hypothesis ($H\pi$) itself is logically derivable from the utility-maximization hypothesis (Hv) under the conditions set out above.

Similarly, when assumption (e) is relaxed, given the others, H_u will no longer imply H_π. For example, being one's own boss, or employing only white workers, are goods that cannot be "consumed" while unemployed, retired, or working for someone else. Consumption of such goods may not be consistent with maximizing profits, though each is chosen voluntarily at some "price."[49] Others have explicitly examined the behavior of firms where some or all of the above assumptions have been relaxed.[50] Their findings largely support the conclusion that deviations from profit maximizing behavior may be explained by the relaxation of some of all five auxiliary assumptions.

Given these considerations, it seems relevant to ask if net revenue maximization (NRM) by union leaders is logically consistent with the Atherton model. Unlike managers in product market firms, union leaders are not subject to pressures from their constituency, or beyond, that would direct their energies toward NRM, other things the same.[51] In the Atherton model, the rank and file members (who may be conceived of as owners of a special type) confront the leadership with pressure that directs it *away from* NRM policies, as discussed above. Thus, if transaction costs are not prohibitive (assumption [d]), rank and file members would make enforceable contracts with leaders *not* to maximize net revenue. Likewise, if there is a market for nonowner management skills (assumption [c]), competition for leadership positions would move leaders toward what Atherton has called the *membership optimum*.

However, and more importantly, consideration of assumptions (a), (b), and (e) is relevant to the net revenue question. If conditions (c) and (d) are relaxed so that rank and file members find it too costly to negotiate enforceable contracts prohibiting NRM, and if officers are insulated from the competitive behavior of would-be leaders, then relaxing conditions (a) and (b) or (e) implies that the utility-maximizing behavior of leaders need not coincide with NRM. In fact, aside from extreme cases in racketeering, which Atherton clearly means to exclude, leaders do not have private-property rights (de jure or de facto) to the residual that is net revenue. Moreover, whatever *stewardship* they enjoy over net receipts, such rights are not transferable for private gain. This suggests that, even if the salaries of union leaders were positively linked to organizational net revenues (so that maximizing the latter meant maximizing the former), leaders would not be expected to pursue NRM policies stressing future receipts. This follows because negotiable rights to future net revenue streams are prohibited and thus cannot be used to offset the uncertainty of leadership tenure, as they are in the conventional theory of the product market firm.[52] Leaders cannot capitalize and appropriate future net receipts streams or salary streams. Therefore, they may be expected to be less interested in maximizing *the net present value of revenues*.

But would the rank and file agree to link leaders' salaries to net revenues in the first place? According to Atherton's model, whether or not dues revenues are independent of members' pecuniary income, NRM need not be coincident with the *membership optimum*. Under these conditions, a policy that rewarded officers directly for deviating from the *membership optimum* would be curious indeed, i.e., illogical.[53] Without the link between leadership salaries and net revenues, NRM will be even less appealing to union management.

This leads to a consideration of (e) above. To the extent that some activities undertaken within the union yield utility to its officers, Atherton suggests that leaders will pursue them with NRM policies.[54] This suggestion apparently confuses income or wealth effects with substitution effects. Other things the same, more revenue at the "disposal" of union leaders undoubtedly allows more of all utility-enhancing elements to be acquired relative to less revenue. But if some of these elements are services provided to members, or inputs in the production of such services, their "consumption" may add to *marginal cost* and thus conflict with maximizing net revenue.[55]

This is a problem that might face the owner of a product market firm with full private-property rights in profits. The cost of "consuming" utility-enhancing resources within the firm is the sacrifice of some profits for use as *general purchasing power*. If these property rights were attenuated, the sacrifice in general purchasing power associated with the same "inefficient" resource use would be lessened, and relatively more of the particular resource would be acquired. If the union's leaders are prohibited from appropriating revenues for nonunion purposes beyond their stated salaries,[56] the costs (in terms of forsaken general purchasing power) of sacrificing net revenues for additional amounts of utility increasing union activities are lower than otherwise, and more than the "optimal" amount of these activities will be undertaken (ceteris paribus). In effect, the limits on the appropriability of net revenues for nonunion activities lowers the relative price of policies that are inconsistent with NRM.

It should be evident from this critique of Atherton's model of union bargaining goals that much of his analysis would have been altered if he had taken notice of the structure of rights facing both members and leaders. The same may be said for economists who have pursued wealth-maximization models of union behavior.

THE WEALTH-MAXIMIZING UNION

Economists who have adopted a wealth maximand for unions have usually suggested either of two alternative models. On the one hand, a union can be thought of as a cartel of wealth-maximizing workers, identical in skill, who hire their leaders to negotiate a simple wage rate per unit of time. The negotiators are constrained, for fear of their jobs, to seek the rate that maximizes the present value of the collective rents of the existing membership. So long as wage rates generate increments in collective income greater than the reservation prices of existing members, the latter will *authorize* wage concessions closer to market clearing levels, since both rents and employment will be raised by them. Beyond some point, however, only employment is increased by further concessions to the employer, and negotiators will not be authorized to agree to them. Where the monopoly wage rate leaves no member unemployed, where opportunity costs are identical, and where supply restrictions are costless, the rents generated through wealth maximization will be distributed equally and optimally among the membership. On the other hand, absent the above assumptions, the pursuit of maximum wealth is beset by obstacles arising from the inevitable competition among the members for scarce jobs and differential rents. Such competition, as in the case of product cartels, threatens the dissipation of collective rents and may give rise to "pooling" arrangements and quota schemes, so familiar in cartel theory, to minimize that threat.[57]

On the other hand, a union can be run to maximize the wealth of its leaders. As long as some *critical* number of members are permitted to keep some *epsilon* of income above their *opportunity costs*, the leadership can maximize its wealth by appropriating the residual associated with a policy of collective rent maximization.[58] Any residual greater than this amount is dangerous to the existence of the leadership's power base. Thus, at both extremes, collective wealth maximization is not threatened by the union's failure to buy and resell labor services; opportunity costs will be revealed in other ways. Nonwealth maximizing behavior, if it exists among unions, must then rest on something other than the objections embraced by the proponents of other theories.

The ownership characteristics associated with union leadership positions were shown to be inconsistent with net revenue maximization in Atherton's model 2. Many of the same considerations may be applied to the wealth maximization models of union behavior discussed above, models that previous writers have summarily, but so inadequately, dismissed.

A recent comprehensive expression of a wealth-maximization model may be found in Powel (1972).[59] Unions create monopoly rents for their incumbent membership by restricting the freedom of individual suppliers of labor services to enter into contracts with employers of union labor. The effect of this prohibition is to raise the supply price of labor above market-clearing levels.[60] The creation of rent results in an excess demand for rent-yielding jobs at the union wage rate. The scarcity of such jobs means that individuals are willing to pay or otherwise devote resources for the right to obtain them. Powel refers to this right as a *job right,* and defines its *value* as the net present value of the monopoly rent to which the job right is attached. Unions are assumed to maximize the value of the job rights they create, which consist of rents associated with the productivity of incumbent members and of rents extracted from the direct or *indirect* sale of job rights to new members.

The Powel model, however, focuses not so much on rent-maximization *via* union wage policy as it does on policies for extracting rents from new members, given the former; a subject largely absent from previous work.[61] Powel demonstrates, and finds some evidence for, the proposition that unions (i.e., incumbent union members) adopt contractual arrangements both with employers and within the membership that either limit the size of the union or establish job quotas so that the value of rights to job access may be appropriated from new members and transfered to incumbents. Moreover, the pricing of job rights is consistent with the hypothesis that the union is a rent-maximizing, discriminating monopolist. Such behavior may take the direct form of discriminatory initiation fees and dues, geared to the differential in expected rent, or the indirect (substitute) form of wage differentials foregone by new members, such as skill and benefit differentials based on seniority.

Powel focuses almost exclusively on the medical profession to test his model and its implications. He concludes that behavior consistent with the pricing of job rights and the transfer of rents by means of price discrimination among members of the profession has been observed. The analogy between the profit-maximizing monopoly producer and the rent-maximizing union, in Powel's analysis, is very strong. He goes on to say, "It appears likely that evidence from other markets would support the generality of the theory" (p. 199). Yet these conclusions are based to an important degree on an auxiliary assumption expressed very early in his analysis. "Incumbent union members, conceptually speaking, are . . . analogous to owners of a firm and may expect to earn a share of the total value of job rights" (p. 1). This view, like the one held by Atherton concerning leaders' *net revenue maximization,* is flawed, both factually and logically, by a failure to appreciate the implications of different ownership forms.

CONCLUSIONS

This analysis suggests that the institutional constraints facing utility-maximizing union officials make it highly unlikely that their behavior will be consistent with the maximization of net revenues from dues receipts or the maximization of monopoly rents for the union. Given these constraints, a single-valued pecuniary maximand ignores a much wider set of utility-affecting variables that are relevant to the welfare of both leaders and members and that imply observable phenomena regarding union activity. The institutional constraints may be characterized as a structure of rights, facing both members and leaders, that define the set of allowable activities for each group. Such rights relate to discretion over the use of resources, monitoring the behavior of other resource users, and appropriating resources for personal uses. As a shorthand expression, the structure of rights associated with a union, or for that matter any organization, may be referred to as its *ownership characteristics*. To a significant degree, this is the one institutional feature that has gone virtually unnoticed by earlier writers searching for a theory of the trade union.

3

An Ownership Profile
of the Trade Union

STUDENTS of labor economics, industrial relations and labor law have spent no small fraction of their time on the description and the discussion of union institutions. There are treatises on union democratic institutions. There are profiles of "the local union" and "the national union" and detailed descriptions of the interrelationships between them. Scholars have exhaustively described trade union internal politics, focusing on the functions of union officers and business agents, and the discontent of rank and file members. Collective bargaining processes and the process of contract ratification have also been examined extensively. Finally, there has been a plethora of books and articles dealing with the effects of federal and state legislation as well as judicial rulings governing trade union goals and activities. This literature has examined the rights of unions as institutions to exist, to secure exclusive bargaining rights, to strike, to boycott, to compete with other unions for members, to collude with employers in restraint of trade, to unilaterally restrain trade, etc. It has also examined the civil rights of members within unions with respect to exercising voting privileges, receiving due process in questions of promotion, discipline, and dismissals, and the fiduciary responsibility of union leaders.

Anyone researching this literature could not but be impressed with its breadth in touching so many elements that constitute the trade union as an institution. Yet, after so much research and analysis over so many years, trade union scholars are still shackled by the complexity and diversity of the institutions they study. There is now so much information about the institutional environment surrounding unions that scholars seem to be unable to abstract a minimal set of institutional characteristics that would permit union behavior to be efficiently modeled and tested against real world experience.

The focus of this book that distinguishes it from others in the field is the emphasis placed on the "ownership characteristics" associated with most labor organizations. It is asserted here that these characteristics contribute substantively to the configuration of constraints that constitute the costs and rewards facing members and leaders, regarding the conduct of union affairs within such organizations and between unions and company management. The task of this chapter is twofold. First, it presents a profile of the union that captures the relevant legal and institutional constraints operating to influence behavior in these organizations. Second, it briefly describes the organizational structure of the union sector and provides a socioeconomic profile of union members.

The following elements constitute a union's "ownership" profile and, unless otherwise stated below, will form the basic set of institutional assumptions underlying the theory of the trade union expressed in chapters five, six, and seven. Trade unions are described by several interesting institutional characteristics.

INSTITUTIONAL CHARACTERISTICS

COLLUSION RIGHTS

1. Unlike nonlabor factor owners, trade unionists are relatively free from liability for conspiracies that result in restraints of trade in labor or product markets, so long as their activities occur within the setting of a labor dispute or in situations where there is a direct employer-employee relationship. However, this exemption from antitrust law is available provided that no conspiracy to restrain trade exists between the employer and the union.[1] This relative immunity from liability under the antitrust laws may be interpreted as a non-transferable right, "owned" by each union member, to engage in labor specific collusive practices including strikes and certain boycotts and picketing. This right makes the cost of joining trade unions relatively lower than other collusions, other things the same.

2. Relative immunity from antitrust legislation, together with several other conditions discussed below, permit, but by no means guarantee, the generation of monopoly rents by labor unions. However, such rents, where they exist, will attract competition from rival unions and would-be unions. This competition will threaten the union with dissipation of monopoly rents, unless it is checked. Moreover, a direct implication from cartel theory suggests that the existence of monopoly rents will make it worthwhile for at least some individual cartel members (in this case, unionists) to cheat on the collusion and for nonmembers to undercut the collusive, or in union jargon, the standard rate. As a consequence, unions will devote resources to monitoring and policing activities affecting their survival and these costs will also threaten rent dissipation, unless otherwise checked. The institution of exclusive bargaining rights is a response to the threat of rent dissipation. Exclusive bargaining rights are "owned" by the union administration as long as it is the certified representative of the firm's employees. The rights impose liability on the employer if he attempts to negotiate with noncertified rivals who wish to negotiate for all or some existing union members during the contract period and between periods.[2] These rights also deny, to members and nonmembers alike, protection from discharge arising out of concerted activities designed to pressure employers into bargaining separately with a minority or them.[3]

Although rivalry among unions can definitely benefit rank and file members, it may also harm them if appropriable rents are dissipated as a result of competition between rivals for rank and file allegiances. Thus, exclusive bargaining rights are a lower cost means of minimizing rent dissipation. Under the National Labor Relations Act, such bargaining rights are transferable by the collective approval of a majority of union members.[4] Where unions are not subject to the National Labor Relations Act or an equivalent state statute, competition for exclusive bargaining rights is manifested by jurisdictional and representational strikes and boycotts that have the effect of securing employer agreement to recognize another bargaining agent. Obviously, this form of competition can be costly and thus rent dissipating.

"SUABILITY"

3. The Labor Management Relations Act (1974, Section 301[a] and 303 [b]) and Rule 17B of the Federal Rules of Civil Procedure

establish that a union may be sued or bring suit as if it were a legal entity. Any money judgment against the union, however, is enforceable only against the organization as an entity and *not* its individual members. Thus individual union members in addition to immunity from antitrust laws, enjoy a form of limited liability from claims against their, almost universally, unincorporated organizations.[5] This should not, however, suggest that individual members are protected from liability for torts or crimes they may commit as union members.

4. Since members of unions are not considered agents of their organization, their actions, unlike the actions of the partners of a firm executing their duties, do not necessarily subject the union to liability. Under the Labor Management Relations Act, however, agency status is not determined by whether the action was authorized or ratified by the membership.[6]

5. The Labor Management Reporting and Disclosure Act of 1959 codifies the common law right of union members to bring civil suit to remedy misapplication of union funds (see Section 501B) in the event of violation of Section 501A, which declares the fiduciary responsibility of union officers. However, the LMRDA imposes requirements on plaintiff members that the common law did not make. Plaintiff members must now request the union itself (or its governing board or officers) to obtain relief by intraunion remedy, within a "reasonable" time before it may seek redress in a federal or state court. Moreover, plaintiff members must show *good cause* before the court will hear their case. The LMRDA also makes theft or embezzlement of union funds or assets by officers a federal crime.[7]

6. Until the Labor Management Relations Act of 1947 and the Labor Management Reporting and Disclosure Act of 1959, there were no federal financial disclosure requirements for unions or their officers nor were there any at common law. However, some states did require some form of disclosure. The LMRA did require financial reports of unions (but not of their officers) who wished to use the offices of the National Labor Relations Board. The later statute, in addition to requiring more detailed versions of the union financial reports under the LMRA, requires that union officers file with the Secretary of Labor an annual report on certain types of conflict of interest holdings or transactions possessed or engaged in by themselves or their families. However, the Act does not expressly outlaw such holdings or transactions nor state that they will be con-

sidered a violation of the fiduciary responsibility that the Act defines in Section 501A.[8]

7. Local unions are not always responsible for their actions. Sometimes their parent or national union may be held responsible. Where the national has *consented* (expressly or implicitly) to unlawful activities by the local, and this consent is in the form of a derived or direct benefit to itself from that action, the parent union may be held liable. Likewise, when a national union has *control*, or the right of control, over a local or intermediate union it may sometimes be liable for the latter's actions. However, "control" in many instances may be vague and liability not clear.[9]

PROPRIETARY INTERESTS

8. Because of their *voluntary association* status, the ownership of property by labor unions[10] is considered to be vested jointly in the membership, or held by the officers in trust for the membership.[11] In the absence of a provision in a union's constitution to the contrary, no member has a severable right to the jointly held property. Upon resignation or lawful expulsion from the union, all rights to such property are lost.

Property division between locals and nationals has been the subject of much litigation since affiliation agreements specify that disaffiliation entitles the national union to the property of the local.[12] However, when a national has been guilty of violating federal law, a disaffiliating local may not lose its property to the parent union.[13] Obviously, one implication that follows from the above property arrangement is that competition for exclusive bargaining rights by rival unions, unaffiliated with the same national, is made more costly.

9. Nothing prevents unions from assigning alienable rights in membership to incumbent members. It is not uncommon for other voluntary associations, such as clubs, to establish, more or less, private-property interests in memberships.[14] Before the New York Stock Exchange incorporated, its voluntary association status was no obstacle to establishing rights to buy and sell seats on the Exchange. Many Pacific-Northwest worker-owned plywood co-ops permit private property in co-op shares. In fact, however, alienable rights to union membership are almost totally absent from labor union history. The only mention of transferable rights in membership I could find referred to a Seattle longshore union at the turn of the century.[15]

A relatively more common but a considerably more attenuated arrangement concerning the alienability of membership rights is found among craft unions and longshoring unions. Incumbent members often bequeath their memberships, upon retirement or death, to immediate relatives.[16] This limited form of transferability is consistent with the view that private property in the membership of large associations makes the monitoring and policing of undesirable member behavior relatively more costly than if admission to the union were more centrally administered. Thus, unions that wish to provide some alienability in membership would restrict the transfer of membership to individuals for whom relatively more knowledge is available.[17]

In most instances full membership in the labor union carries with it voting rights relevant to internal union government. However, unlike the voting rights owned by shareholders of a corporation, union voting rights, because memberships are not transferable, may not be accumulated. Policy and leadership changes, therefore, become relatively more costly where ownership rights are inalienable. In many respects, the ownership rights associated with mutual savings and loan associations or insurance companies are closely analogous to the ownership rights found in most conventional trade unions.[18]

PARTICIPATION RIGHTS

10. Until relatively recently, voluntary association status has protected union admission policies from the scrutiny of the courts. It has not been uncommon for craft or referral unions to ration membership by race, sex, nationality and even religion. Industrial unions, rather than attempt exclusionary admission policies, have rationed employment opportunities and income earning opportunities by adopting segregated union chapters, segregated apprenticeship programs and segregated seniority lists.[19]

Beginning with the Railway Labor Act, legal restrictions on union admission policies were based upon protection of the employee's "right to work," where union membership is a condition of employment, and/or on protection of the employee's "right to participate," where the union's policies directly affect *all* workers of a particular class without regard to union membership. Where unions can show that discriminatory admission policies do not affect access to work, such policies have not been attacked by the courts. In Oliphant vs. Brotherhood of Local Firemen (262 F. 2d 359 6 Circuit 1958) a Federal Court of Appeals ruled that neither the provisions of the Railway Labor Act nor the Constitution required the Railway Brotherhood to admit blacks to membership in the absence of any claim of discrimination in *representation.* The only participation guaranteed by the act, the court ruled, was the initial right to vote for a bargaining representative, and the provisions of the Constitution were inapplicable because no government action was involved. The Labor Management Reporting and Disclosure Act, while treating participation in union activities, does not affect union admission policies directly.

11. Before the Labor Management Reporting and Disclosure Act, the constitution and bylaws of many unions distinguished between different classes of members as to the degree to which they could participate in union government and benefits. Nominating and voting for officers or seeking candidacy were often not extended to apprentice and semiskilled members. Unless litigating members could demonstrate the denial of a property right or the violation of a civil right under the U.S. Constitution, many courts would not hear cases that complained of discriminatory treatment within unions.[20] At the federal level differential participation rights in union activities were tolerated by the federal courts under the Taft-Hartley Act so long as it could not be demonstrated that these practices barred affected members and nonmembers from access to jobs under the collective bargaining agreement. Under the LMRDA, every member in good standing has equal rights and privileges within the organization to nominate candidates, to vote in elections or referendums, and to attend membership meetings, *subject to reasonable rules and regulations established by the organization's constitution and bylaws.*[21]

The LMRDA also prescribes maximum intervals between elections of union officers at national, intermediate, and local union levels. Any member *after having exhausted available intraunion remedies* or having failed to obtain a final decision after three months of invoking those remedies, may file a complaint with the Secretary of Labor. The Secretary is then empowered to bring civil action against the union in a federal district court. The court may then direct an election under the supervision of the Secretary of Labor. The exhaustion of remedies requirement, which did not exist at common law, may have the effect of raising the cost of challenging irregular activities within unions.[22] Note also that the Labor Management Reporting and Disclosure Act does not affect existing rights and remedies to enforce the constitution and bylaws of a labor organization with respect to *pending* elections. It is applicable only *ex post*.

In response to the advantage incumbent officers have had in the past in running for re-election, the LMRDA requires that the union comply with "reasonable" requests to distribute the campaign literature of all candidates at their own expense, and that it refrain from discriminating among candidates with respect to the use of membership lists and with respect to authorization for expenditures on campaign literature. Also, no union funds may be contributed to promote the candidacy of any person, though such funds may be used for the publication of notices, factual statements of issues not involving candidates, and other expenses necessary for holding the election.

EXHAUSTION OF REMEDIES

12. Consistent with the common law's reluctance to interfere in the internal affairs of voluntary associations, litigants claiming that they have been harmed by union actions inconsistent with the constitution and by-laws of their organization have been required to exhaust all intraunion remedies before they approach the court. Only in those cases dealing with financial irregularities in union activities have the courts waived the exhaustion rule. The Labor Management Reporting and Disclosure Act goes one step further and, except for misapplication of union funds, requires that the exhaustion rule be waived after a four month lapse in time where no action has been taken by the union. The effect of this provision is to remove procrastination as a strategy by unions unwilling to adjudicate claims made by their own members.[23]

NONPROFIT STATUS

13. Under the Internal Revenue Service code, labor unions may qualify as nonprofit organizations. Revenues from initiation fees, dues, earnings from investments, and other sources of revenue earned by the union as an institution are exempt from income and capital gains taxation. With no other residual claimants, the union must employ net revenue to the benefit of the collective membership. This may take the form of administrative services, union-provided collective benefits for the membership (such as recreation

facilities), the purchase of assets in the union's name but jointly held by the membership, and retained earnings in the form of demand deposits at commercial banks. Nonprofit status brings with it other privileges including subsidized postal services. Until the Labor Management Reporting and Disclosure Act, it was not illegal for union officers to own profit-making firms that serviced the nonprofit union. This is not uncommon outside unions; the executives of other voluntary associations, such as savings and loan associations, often own for-profit companies that sell services to the nonprofit institutions.[24]

STRUCTURAL CHARACTERISTICS

If institutional constraints, such as those profiled in this chapter, are determinants of union behavior, it may not be unreasonable to conjecture that they also contribute to the determination of the size distribution of unions and other dimensions of union structure.

Although this conjecture is only briefly examined in the chapters that follow, it seems appropriate here to provide the reader with a structural profile of the union sector without concerning ourselves with the causal elements that might explain its particular shape. The purpose of this profile is to familiarize the reader with descriptive statistics about American national and international unions.

THE STRUCTURE OF THE UNION SECTOR

The exact number of union and unionlike organizations in the United States is not known with certainty. However, the Bureau of Labor Statistics reports, most recently[25], that there were 175 national and international labor unions and 37 employee associations headquartered in the United States and known to be interstate in scope. These organizations claimed a total membership of 24.2 million.[26] Conventional labor unions claimed 89 percent of this figure, or 21.6 million persons.

Most union members, however, are more familiar with their local organizations within the nationals. In 1974 labor union membership was distributed among 69,468 affiliated locals. Although no systematic tally of local unions *unaffiliated* with nationals and internationals is regularly produced, a 1967 Bureau survey revealed that there were 884 such organizations and that they represented

475,000 members, or 2.3 percent of the 1974 U.S. union membership estimate.[27]

The AFL-CIO (American Federation of Labor–Congress of Industrial Organizations) is a policy-making federation of 108 nationals and internationals that performs lobbying, research and intraunion arbitration services such as those relevant to jurisdictional disputes between member unions. The AFL-CIO claims 16.9 million members, or 78 percent of total union membership. The 64 nationals and internationals unaffiliated with the AFL-CIO reported membership equal to 4.7 million persons and were distributed among 10,191 locals.

Neither membership nor collective bargaining activities are distributed proportionately among national unions. For example, roughly 67 percent of the 195,000 collective bargaining agreements that were in effect in 1974 were negotiated by nine unions.[28] See table 1. These unions claimed roughly a third of all union membership. Conversely, 105 national unions negotiated a total of only 4,806 contracts in the same year. Tables 2 and 3 help explain this phenomenon. Table 2 displays the distribution of national unions by number of local unions. Over 50 percent of local unions are affiliated with 16 national unions, which is less than 10 percent of those nationals reporting to the Bureau. This suggests a significant degree of concentration, since the number of collective agreements is correlated with the number of union locals. Table 3 represents the distribution of national unions by membership size. Almost 60 percent of estimated union membership is concentrated in 16 national unions. Conversely, 82 unions, almost 50 percent of all national unions, represented only 2.2 percent of all union members. This heavy concentration of membership and union locals in relatively few national labor organizations has become a prominent characteristic of organized labor in the twentieth century.[29] Table 4 presents a list of the largest 9 national and international unions by membership. Note that almost 75 percent of the 4.7 million members located in the 64 independent nationals are represented by the two largest unions in the country, the Teamsters and the United Automobile Workers, respectively.

Finally, union membership growth has not kept pace with labor force growth, although both have grown absolutely. Table 5 traces the decline in union representation in the labor force over the last two decades. However, the decline is less dramatic if account is taken of the growth in employee associations since 1968.[30]

TABLE 1

Distribution of National Unions by Number of Basic Bargaining Agreements with Employers, 1974[a]

Number of Agreements	All unions		Agreements		AFL-CIO		Unaffiliated	
	Number	Percent	Number	Percent	Unions	Agreements	Unions	Agreements
All unions[b]	172	100.0	194,726	100.0	108	146,589	64	48,137
No agreements[c]	4	2.3	-	-	-	-	4	-
Less than 25	53	30.8	344	2	16	107	37	237
25 and under 100	25	14.5	1,336	7	14	798	11	538
100 and under 200	23	13.4	3,126	1.6	19	2,591	4	535
200 and under 300	9	5.2	2,292	1.2	8	2,008	1	284
300 and under 500	11	6.4	4,234	2.2	8	3,231	3	1,003
500 and under 1,000	15	8.7	10,500	5.4	14	9,760	1	740
1,000 and under 2,000	15	8.7	18,889	9.7	14	17,389	1	1,500
2,000 and under 3,000	3	1.7	6,300	3.2	6,300	-	-	-
3,000 and under 5,000	5	2.9	17,750	9.1	4	14,450	1	3,300
5,000 and over	9	5.2	129,955	66.7	8	39,955	1	40,000

[a]The number of basic collective bargaining agreements does not include various supplements or pension, health, and welfare agreements as separate documents.

[b]Includes 36 unions for which the Bureau estimated the number of basic collective bargaining agreements. For 3 unions—the Hotel and Restaurant Employees and Bartenders International Union (AFL-CIO), the Amalgamated Clothing Workers of America (AFL-CIO) and the Pattern Makers League of North America (AFL-CIO), sufficient information was not available on which to base an estimate.

[c]Though 4 unions report an absence of a collective bargaining agreement, this situation is a permanent characteristic of only the National Association of Postal Supervisors (Ind.) and the National League of Postmasters of the United States (Ind.). Both of these unions represent government employees. The National Hockey League Players' Association (Ind.) and the National Football League Players' Association (Ind.) usually have such agreements but were without one at the time these data were collected.

Source: Directory of National Unions and Employee Associations, 1975. B.L.S. 1977

TABLE 2

DISTRIBUTION OF NATIONAL UNIONS AND EMPLOYEE ASSOCIATIONS BY NUMBER OF LOCALS AND OTHER SUBORDINATE BODIES, 1974

Number of locals or chapters	All unions		Locals		AFL-CIO		Unaffiliated		Associations	
	Number	Percent	Number	Percent	Unions	Locals	Unions	Locals	Number	Chapters
Total[a]	175	100.0	69,468	100.0	111	59,277	64	10,191	37	14,825
Under 10[b]	31	17.7	70	.1	8	20	23	50	5	25
25 and under 50	16	9.1	564	.8	9	307	7	257	5	173
50 and under 100	20	11.4	1,390	2.0	13	993	7	397	8	495
100 and under 200	16	9.1	2,238	3.2	12	1,641	4	597	2	499
200 and under 300	17	9.7	4,103	5.9	17	4,103	–	–	2	420
300 and under 400	7	4.0	2,431	3.5	7	2,431	–	–	–	–
400 and under 500	9	5.1	3,977	5.7	8	3,527	1	450	–	–
500 and under 600	3	1.7	1,585	2.3	2	1,085	1	500	–	–
600 and under 700	6	3.4	3,847	5.5	6	3,847	–	–	–	–
700 and under 800	5	2.9	3,733	5.4	4	2,954	1	779	–	–
800 and under 900	6	3.4	5,075	7.3	4	3,420	2	1,655	–	–
900 and under 1,000	2	1.1	1,884	2.7	2	1,884	–	–	1	900
1,000 and under 1,500	3	1.7	3,573	5.1	3	3,573	–	–	2	2,396
1,500 and under 2,000	7	4.0	12,003	17.3	5	8,723	2	3,280	–	–
2,000 and over	6	3.4	22,671	32.6	5	20,671	1	2,000	1	9,745

[a] 7 unions and 1 association did not report the number of subordinates, but sufficient information was avilable on which to base estimates for these organizations. Also included were 5,070 locals outside the United States.
[b] Includes 16 unions and 1 association that have no locals.

Source: Directory of National Unions and Employee Associations, 1975. B.L.S. 1977.

TABLE 3

DISTRIBUTION OF NATIONAL UNIONS BY SIZE OF ORGANIZATION, 1974

Size of Organization	Unions Total		Members		AFL-CIO
	Number	Percent	Number (thousand)	Percent	
Total[a]	175	100.0	21,585	100.0	111
Under 1,000 members	26	14.9	9	(b)	6
1,000 and under 5,000	26	14.9	71	.3	6
5,000 and under 10,000	9	5.1	61	.3	6
10,000 and under 25,000	21	12.0	337	1.6	16
25,000 and under 50,000	27	15.4	931	4.3	21
50,000 and under 100,000	18	10.3	1,281	5.9	14
100,000 and under 200,000	20	11.4	2,869	13.3	17
200,000 and under 300,000	9	5.1	2,233	10.3	8
300,000 and under 400,000	3	1.7	981	4.5	3
400,000 and under 500,000	5	2.9	2,215	10.3	5
500,000 and under 1,000,000	8	4.6	5,779	26.8	8
1,000,000 and over	3	1.7	4,818	22.3	1

[a]See footnote a, table 2.
[b]Less than 0.05 percent.

Note: Because of rounding, sums of individual items may not equal total.

Source: Directory of National Unions and Employee Associations, 1975. B.L.S. 1977.

TABLE 4

9 LARGEST TRADE UNIONS [a]

Organization [b]	Members [c]
Unions: Teamsters	1,973,000
Automobile Workers (Ind.)	1,545,000
Steelworkers	1,300,000
Electrical (IBEW)	991,000
Machinists	943,000
Carpenters	820,000
Retail Clerks	651,000
Laborers	650,000
State, County	550,000

[a]Based on union and association reports to the Bureau with membership rounded to the nearest thousand. All unions not identified as (Ind.) are affiliated with the AFL-CIO.

[b]For mergers and changes in affiliation since 1972, see Appendix A.

[c]Membership estimated by the Bureau and not available for publication.

Source: Directory of National Unions and Employee Associations, 1975. B.L.S. 1977.

WHO JOINS UNIONS?

A profile of union members by socioeconomic characteristics reveals them to be distinguishable from their nonunion counterparts. For example, the median age of union members, according to a B.L.S. report in 1970, was forty-one, five years above that of nonunion workers.[31] The median earnings of a full-time union worker in 1970 averaged $1,157 higher than a "comparable" nonunion worker.[32] Union workers are more likely to be found in blue-collar jobs than white-collar jobs. Blue-collar union members are more likely to be craftsmen than operatives and laborers respectively. Almost 36 percent of black blue-collar workers were union members, while 40 percent of whites in this occupational category were union members. Still the extent of unionization among black workers was greater than for whites in most occupations. Nearly 22 percent of black wage and salary workers belonged to unions in 1970, compared with 20 percent of white workers.[33] Among durable goods industries, the disparity ranges between 47 percent participation by blacks and 36 percent participation by whites.[34]

TABLE 5

National Union Membership as a Proportion of Labor
Force and Nonagricultural Employment, 1958–74 [a]

(Numbers in Thousands)

Year	Membership excluding Canada	Total labor force		Employees in nonagricultural establishments	
		Number	Percent members	Number	Percent members
Unions:					
1958	17,029	70,275	25.2	51,363	33.2
1959	17,117	70,921	24.1	53,313	32.1
1960	17,049	72,142	23.6	54,234	31.4
1961	16,303	73,031	22.3	54,042	30.2
1962	16,586	73,442	22.6	55,596	29.8
1963	16,524	74,571	22.2	56,702	29.1
1964	16.841	75,830	22.2	[b] 58,331	28.9
1965	17,299	77,178	22.4	60,815	28.4
1966	17,940	78,893	22.7	63,955	28.1
1967	18,367	80,793	22.7	65,857	27.9
1968	18,916	82,272	23.0	[b] 67,951	[b] 27.8
1969	19,036	82,240	22.6	[b] 70,442	[b] 27.0
1970	19,381	85,903	22.6	[b] 70,920	[b] 27.3
1971	19,211	86,929	22.1	[b] 71,222	[b] 27.0
1972	19,435	88,991	21.8	[b] 73,714	[b] 26.4
1973	19,851	91,040	21.8	76,896	25.8
1974	20,199	93,240	21.7	78,413	25.8

[a] Totals include reported membership and directly affiliated local union members. Total reported Canadian membership and members of single-firm unions are excluded.

[b] Revised.

Source: Directory of National Unions and Employee Associations, 1975. B.L.S. 1977

This may reflect relatively lower valued nonunion alternatives for blacks, on the one hand, and relatively greater opportunities for whites in managerial and administrative jobs that have been less amenable to unionization, on the other. A notable exception to the participation disparities is the construction industry where almost 40 percent of white wage and salary workers belong to unions and only 33 percent of black workers are members.[35]

Participation in unions by women is only 10.3 percent of their numbers in industry, and, except for public administration and private welfare, it is everywhere smaller than male participation.[36] Moreover, participation disparities are even greater between black (13.8) and white (9.8) women than between their male counterparts.[37]

To summarize, the representative union member is a white male, 41 years old, employed in a blue-collar occupation in the manufacturing sector and earning between 10 and 13 percent more than his nonunion counterparts.

4

The Basic Model in a Proprietary Paradigm

THE underlying theme or message that should surface from the critique in chapter two is the importance of identifying, a priori, the circumstances in which a given maximand is relevant to trade union behavior. This is so whether attention is focused on the maximization of wealth, the wage bill, the average wage rate, net revenues, membership growth, or utility; or whether maximizing is replaced by "satisficing."[1] It is argued here that the relevant criteria for identifying appropriate maximands are the *configuration of members' rights* over the use of and yield from union resources in conjunction with members' labor services; and the cost of enforcing that configuration, where such rights are defined by the *ownership characteristics* of unions, including the laws that regulate them. The array of institutional elements that constitute these ownership characteristics and that shape the constraints within which unions and their leaders pursue objectives were discussed in chapter three.

The role of the trade union in society is often described in multidimensional terms. It is at once economic, fraternal, political, egalitarian, revolutionary, and educational. Yet, none can doubt that the source of its ability to serve these roles is its comparative advantage in affecting the terms of trade (both pecuniary and nonpecuniary) in the labor market. This capacity derives from the legally sanctioned, publicly and privately enforced restriction on the contractual freedom of all individuals who would otherwise supply labor services competitively to employers of union members.[2] These restrictions are defined by the *exclusivity* of bargaining rights held by the union within some specified jurisdiction.[3] As the sole bargaining agent for its members, the union is not only insulated from the competition of rival unions' representational claims (and the demands such claims would make on resources), but also from the threat to the collective posed by the independent bargains otherwise struck between employers and individual union members. In this sense, an exclusive bargaining right is a resource that facilitates the exercise of collusive behavior among workers, i.e., monopoly.

Together with the strike (the ability to effectively and legally withhold competitive labor services from a given employer), exclusive bargaining rights make the union an instrument for the production of monopoly rents that may be appropriated by its patron-owners—the members. These rents are created by getting employers to agree to pecuniary and nonpecuniary compensations that exceed those available at market-clearing terms.

CONTROLLING COMPENSATING MARGINS

Any employment relationship, union or otherwise, is multidimensional. There is a wage rate, the worker's productive abilities, the physical working conditions, the quality and number of complementary human and nonhuman resources, the personalities of the parties to the relationship, and so on. Almost all of these elements are amenable to adjustment at the margin. The more elements and the greater the extent to which the employer is free to adjust at the margin, the less valuable is the union's "exclusive" bargaining right. That is, the fewer the elements over which it has exclusive rights in the employment relationship the less valuable are the set of rights it does possess.

The acquisition of an exclusive bargaining right per se does not ordinarily include the requirement that employees belong to the union or that membership be a precondition of employment, or that remission of fees to the union be a condition of continued employment, or that promotion and layoff be associated with union-seniority status.[4] Thus, in the absence of additional arrangements, employers can make adjustments on a number of margins that have the effect of minimizing the rents that unions would otherwise appropriate for themselves. This suggests that, in addition to sole representation, the value of bargaining rights is enhanced by mechanisms that would increase the union's control over the other margins on which employers make adjustments.

One means to this end would be a detailed specification of the allowable discretion employers may exercise in their contacts with workers and in the productive process itself. Specifications that enhance the monitoring of worker competitiveness, skills, union loyalty, and of personal characteristics that might affect union "solidarity" as well as specifications relating to the labor composition of productive processes, either have found their way into collective agreements, or have otherwise acquired a de facto degree of legitimacy.[5] However, with so many margins to cover, specifying "do's and don'ts" may be particularly costly for the union to police and enforce. This is especially true of one-on-one relationships between the employer and a specific worker.

As an alternative means to such detailed specifications, the closed and union shops promise lower cost monitoring powers for the union over individual employee-employer behavior. Both of these institutions have long been recognized for their contributions to "union security," providing solutions to free-rider problems that plague the collective good outputs of unions.[6] The closed shop has most often been viewed as a supply restricting, wage-lifting device that simultaneously rations scarce, "high" priced jobs among surplus workers.[7] But, in the context of this chapter, the closed shop is also a device for screening out workers who would threaten the monopoly potential of the union. Moreover, both types of shops, union and closed, are in a strategic position to punish members who cooperate with employers on margins not expressly covered in formal agreements. Members who behave in a manner which threatens the collusive interests of their union may be, and have been, fined, suspended and expelled from such organizations. In the latter case, the union can bring pressure on the firm to discharge or otherwise monetarily penalize the expelled member.[8]

Sometimes the function of policing free riders coincides with that of protecting against the employer's use of uncovered margins, as in the case of strike and picket services required to secure the collective benefits of union activity. Exclusive bargaining rights together with an *agency shop*, for example, would only relieve the free-rider problem to the extent that *all* employees, union and nonunion, covered by the collective agreement were required to pay dues (or a fee in lieu of dues) to the union. "Payments" in the form of strike and picketing services, however, which contribute to collective benefits and which are not automatically collected by the union would still leave the free rider in the saddle. Likewise, to the extent that nonunion employees can be persuaded to strike and picket, it may be in the employer's interest, *at the margin*, to devote resources to dissuading them from such activities. Closed and union shops, with their superior disciplinary weapons, can thus effectively, though no longer legitimately, seal off this margin to the employer by limiting employment opportunities for nonunion workers and by threatening the jobs of members who seek a free ride in the strike and picket dimensions. In this case, although the *shops* simultaneously constrain the free rider and shut off another margin to the employer, these two activities are clearly separate.[9] Innovations such as these alter the value of bargaining rights and make the rights themselves *more* exclusive.[10]

RENT PRODUCTION AND COMPOSITION[11]

Union monopoly rents may be expressed in a variety of pecuniary and nonpecuniary forms, reflected both in the collectively bargained remuneration package and in the services provided directly to members by the union itself.[12] Because the firm sometimes has a comparative advantage in providing some on-the-job or job-connected goods which are consumed or used by its workers, the employer is not indifferent to the composition of the remuneration package exchanged for labor services. This suggests that in addition to the "normal" cost unions face in attempting to improve their terms of trade with employers, the latter will offer differential resistance to alternative remuneration packages of equal *market* value. Resistance may take the form of prolonged negotiation, or willingness to sustain longer strikes, or perhaps just lethargy in executing an agreement once it is signed. This, of course, implies added costs for the union. Some remuneration packages for which it might bargain will be more costly to secure and thus yield smaller rents than others.

We define the real value of union rents appropriable to (though not necessarily by) incumbent members as ϱ_r. This is the present value of the residual that is the difference between the discounted sum of pecuniary and nonpecuniary differentials resulting from the exercise of union monopoly power and the value of resources committed by the union, on behalf of its members, in supplying collective bargaining services to the latter.[13] It is the wealth of the incumbent membership.

Where,

$$\varrho_T = [\bar{W}(\overline{mH})/P* - \hat{W}(\overline{mH})/P* + (P_1G_1) - P_1'G_1' - FX] \qquad (1)$$

And:

$\bar{W}$ = A vector of discounted *contract* nominal wage rates containing ($\bar{w}_i$) wage rates over (n) time periods.

$\overline{mH}$ = Contract manhours. The product of contract employment for members, m, and contract hours, $\bar{H}$, a vector containing $\bar{h}_i$ hours per worker-member discounted over (n) time periods.

$P*$ = Price deflator

$\hat{W}$ = A vector composed of discounted *market* clearing nominal wage rates $\hat{w}_i$, or wage rates in best alternatives, over (n) time periods.[14]

P_1G_1 = A vector of discounted market values composed of g_j goods, valued at discounted p_i prices (p_jg_j) produced by union or firm under collective agreement and consumed by members *on the job*.

$P_1'G_1'$ = A vector of discounted market values composed of g_j' goods, valued at discounted p_j' prices ($p_j'g_j'$). produced by the firm and consumed by employees *on the job without union contract*.

F = A vector composed of discounted resource prices f_i faced by the union in producing rents over n time periods.

X = A vector composed of resources x_i employed by the union in seeking rents over n time periods.

n = Number of periods during which rents will be received.

Given that rents are composed of both pecuniary and nonpecuniary payments, their magnitudes are, in part, a function of the particular selection of W and G_1 made by the union, and of employer resistance associated with some selections. The production of rents is subject to the following constraints:

$$\beta(\bar{W}, G_1) = Z(X) \qquad (2)$$

$$-\frac{dmH}{d\bar{W}} \cdot \frac{\bar{W}}{mH} = \eta \qquad (3)$$

where (2) is a rent production function for all goods identified with rents, including the vector of those goods (G_o) that general purchasing power will buy outside the firm and union. We substitute $(\bar{W})$ in (2) since the union affects members' command over (G_o) through this variable. Equation (3) is a "wage" elasticity of labor demand in terms of man-hours for members. More accurately (3) may be interpreted as a *variable labor cost elasticity of labor* demand to call attention to the fact that remuneration per man-hour includes variable nonwage payments as well.[15]

Rent creation by the union implies a relative scarcity of jobs, at the union wage, to those seeking employment or wishing to retain it in the unionized firm. The scarcity value of these jobs depends in part on the form(s) in which rents may be appropriated. Under closed shop or even union shop conditions, membership effectively represents an access right to employment. If rights to rent-yielding jobs, *job rights*, were assigned individually to incumbent members (e.g., in the form of union cards or positions in the hiring queue) and both specified and enforced as their *alienable property*, the cost to members of endorsing rent-affecting policies that *failed* to maximize the net present value of a job right would be greater than if transferability were prohibited.[16] This follows because transfer rights imply the possibility of immediate capitalization and appropriation of expected future rents into the present, while an absence of such rights implies that rents can only be appropriated when and where they are generated. Unless life span and job tenure are known with certainty and the individual member does not plan to change employers, *nontransferability* suggests a lower opportunity cost to individual members of ignoring the future consequences of present collective action. To the extent that such actions affect the production of rent, it will be less costly than otherwise to ignore them for other activities.

Members can receive rents directly from their wages, from the transfer of their membership to others (where permitted or not policed), and from the nonpecuniary goods and services they consume on the job. Rents may *also* be acquired by members as dividends, where unions distribute "surplus" receipts (from initiation fees and dues) over and above the costs of providing union services such as collective bargaining. Members are *residual claimants* in that the size of rents, whatever their form or method of distribution, are affected by the costs (dues, strike support, boycott support, etc.) members sustain to acquire them.[17]

CHOICES AFFECTING UTILITY

Since most workers must be physically present on the job in order to deliver their work, the working environment (in both its tangible and intangible forms) is a source of utility to them, *irrespective of the nature of their ownership rights in the union.* Purely as a matter of taste, the set of utility-maximizing environmental characteristics for any given worker could be different from the set that maximizes rents. These characteristics include many of the nonpecuniary goods, G_1, that contribute to the composition of rents in (1) above; such as plant or office lighting and air conditioning, work tools, personal characteristics of co-workers, cafeteria menus, work clothes, etc. This suggests that, where members can affect union decisions, a model that accommodates preferences will yield a richer set of implications.[18] Toward this end, we introduce a twice differentiable utility function for a representative member.[19]

$$U_m = U(G_o, G_1) = U_m(g_i \ldots, g_j \ldots) \tag{4}$$

Members derive utility from two classes of goods, G_o and G_1. The vector, G_o, represents goods consumed off the job and acquired through general purchasing power (i.e., real wage payments).[20] These are goods individuals purchase with $\bar{w}(\bar{h})m/P^*$ real income. If we assume that both $\bar{h}$ (the worker's contract hours) and P^* (the price level) are exogenous to the individual union member, and if we assume that relative prices among g_i elements in G_o are fixed, so that G_o may be treated as a Hicksian *composite good*, then members' choices between off-the-job consumption, G_o, and on-the-job consumption, G_1, reflect choices between g_j elements of the latter vector and $\bar{w}$, the contract nominal wage rate sought by the union member. Given the constraints faced by union members, utility-maximizing choices by individuals, as expressed through a collective choice procedure, will yield unique values for nominal wage rates and G_1.[21] We take as axiomatic that members behave as if they maximized utility irrespective of the ownership characteristics of their particular organization.

For each member the choice theoretic structure that bears on union policy objectives may be written in expected utility form:[22]

$$\text{MAX } \phi = \theta u_m (G_o, G_1) + (1 - \theta) \, u_m (G'_o, G'_1) = \tag{5}$$
$$\theta u_m (g_i..., g_j...) + (1-\theta) \, u_m (g_i..., g_j...)$$

Subject to:

$$0 \leqslant \theta \leqslant 1 \tag{5.1}$$

$$\text{and } (P_o G_o)_m + (P_1 G_1)_m \leqslant \varrho_m + (\hat{w}\hat{h})_m + (P_1 G_1)_m + Y_m \tag{5.2}$$

if the union job is retained or

$$(P'_o G'_o)_m + (P'_1 G'_1)_m \leqslant (\hat{w}\hat{h})_m + Y_m \tag{5.3}$$

if the union job is abolished

where $\varrho_m = \delta \varrho_T$

Recall that $\varrho_T = \{\bar{W}(\overline{mH})/P^* - \hat{W}(\overline{mH})/P^* + (P'_1 G'_1 - P_1 G_1) - FX\}$ (1)

and that 1. $G_o = Z(X)$

2. $G_1 = Z(X)$

$$\text{or } \beta (G_0 G_1) = Z(X) \tag{2}$$

The symbol θ in (5) is the probability that a given card holder will retain his job, over some specified period as a result of union policy objectives. $(1 - \theta)$ is the probability that he will be in a non-union job as a result of collective bargaining. θ is a function of the variable cost (or wage) elasticity of demand for labor, the percentage increase in variable cost attributable to union labor, and the seniority of the card holder.[23]

In expression (5.2), the constraint faced by a utility-maximizing worker under union contract includes the variable ϱ_m. This is the net present value of the stream of rents appropriable to any given union member, and $\varrho_m = \delta \varrho_T$. If all employed members share rents equally, $\delta = 1/m$. It is more likely, however, that older and more skilled members enjoy a higher δ than younger and less skilled members. $(\hat{w}\hat{h})_m$ is the segment of a member's total wage earnings attributable to competitive opportunity costs at union contract hours $\hat{h}$. Likewise, $(P'_1 G'_1)_m$ is the segment of nonpecuniary benefits that are obtained in competitive markets. In (5.3), the constraint faced by a worker not under union contract, $(\hat{w}\hat{h})_m$ represents his earnings and hours under competitive conditions. The variable Y_m in both (5.2) and (5.3), respectively, is other income.

If we assume that θ is exogenous to the worker's choice decision, then G'_o and G'_1 may be taken as exogenous also, since they are determined for the worker by the competitive sector of the labor market. Therefore, under this assumption, the choice problem facing the individual member is to maximize just $\theta u(G_o, G_1)$ in (5) subject to (5.1) and (5.2).

$$\text{Max } \phi = \theta u_m(G_o, G_1) = \theta u_m(G_o, g_j \ldots) \tag{5'}$$
$$\text{S.T. } (5.1)$$
$$(5.2)$$

Using the Lagragian procedure

$$\text{max } \phi = \theta u_m(G_o, G_1) - \lambda[P_oG_o + P_1G_1 - \varrho_m - \hat{w}h/P^* - P_1'G_1' - Y]$$

First order conditions in G_0, a Hicksian composite good, and G_1 are:

$$d\phi/dG_o = \theta \partial u/\partial G_o - \lambda[P_o - \partial \varrho_m/\partial G_o] = 0 \tag{5.4}$$
$$d\phi/dg_j = \theta \partial u/\partial g_j - \lambda[p_j - \partial_m/\partial g_j] = 0^{24} \tag{5.5}$$

The first order condition in (5.4) identifies the effective price for the marginal unit of the composite good G_o. This is $P_o - \partial \varrho_m/\partial G_o$. The effective price of a marginal unit of the g_j good in the vector G_1, as defined in (5.5), is $p_j - \partial \varrho_m/\partial g_j$. Between G_0 and the jth good in the G_1 vector, utility is maximized where

$$\theta \partial u/\partial g_j \big/ \theta \partial u/\partial G_o = p_j - \partial \varrho_m/\partial g_j \big/ P_o - \partial \varrho_m/\partial G_o \tag{6}$$

This expression is a variant of the conventional condition for utility maximization. Conventionally, the ratio of marginal utilities of any two goods must equal the ratio of their prices. To the extent that the choice of g_j increases the rent generated by union activity so that $\partial \varrho_m/\partial g_j > 0$, the *effective price* of choosing more g_j is lower than its ostensible price p_j. Imagine g_j to be cafeteria lunches at the work place. The average price for such a lunch is p_j. Assume, however, that the union would be successful in bargaining for a higher quality lunch than would obtain in the absence of a union contract, i.e., than if the quality of lunches were determined by competitive market forces alone. The higher quality lunch, at p_j, is a nonpecuniary rent, the value of which must be deducted from the ostensible price p_j to reflect the effective price of consuming a cafeteria lunch at work. Consumption will proceed until the marginal utility of consuming lunch equals this effective price. As $\partial \varrho_m/\partial g_j$ increases, the effective price of g_j falls, ceteris paribus. Likewise, a fall in $\partial \varrho_m/\partial g_j$ will *raise* the effective price of g_j. When $\partial \varrho_m/\partial g_j = 0$, the price of this good is p_j and utility maximization requires its equality with $\partial u/\partial g_j$.

For some goods, g_n the *ostensible* price facing the individual union member at the margin will be zero. These are public goods. For example, plant lighting is an object of collective bargaining and a potential source of nonpecuniary rent to the representative union member. Yet, the ostensible price of consuming another unit of candlepower will be zero to him. The effective price facing this member is therefore $-\partial \varrho_m / \partial g_n$, the increment in rent associated with another unit of candlepower in the plant. Rent as a function of candlepower is subject to diminishing marginal returns. Therefore, the more candlepower demanded, the lower $\partial \varrho_m / \partial g_n$. At some level of g_n, $|\partial \varrho_m / \partial g_n| < 0$ and the effective price facing the union member will be *positive*. Utility will be maximized at $\partial u / \partial g_m = -\partial \varrho_m / \partial g_n$. This will occur where $-\partial \varrho_m / \partial g_n \geqslant 0$.

The above analysis is also relevant for treating variations in the Hicksian composite good, G_o, the vector of goods that a union member consumes off the job with real earnings and at constant relative prices. If we continue to assume that P^* and $\hbar$ are exogenous to members, an increase in members' demands for G_o or in the quantity of G_o demanded, translates into a demand for higher wage rates, $\bar{W}$, or general purchasing power. For any given union member, under a collective agreement, a wage increase will appear as if it were a public good, i.e., the ostensible "price" of securing that increase is zero for him.[25] Moreover, as long as the increment in $\bar{w}$ adds to his share of union rent (i.e., $\partial \varrho_m / \partial \bar{w} > 0$) he will be able to increase his consumption of G_o. By choosing to consume more G_o, until $\partial u / \partial G_o = -\partial \varrho_m / \partial G_o$, the union member will select a contract wage rate that maximizes his utility. Thus, constrained utility maximizing for a representative member, by choice of G_o and G_1, implies a unique set of wage and nonwage bargaining goals. Those goals may be modified by changes in any of the elements in the effective prices that members face, including the implicit elements that determine real earnings, i.e., P^* and $\hbar$.

A PROPRIETARY PARADIGM

It will be useful, for later analyses, to examine at this point the relatively rare case of the proprietary trade union. This is the case where union members have private, transferable property rights in access to union membership and indirectly to rent-yielding jobs. Unions that allow members to bequeath their union cards to heirs (e.g., some East Coast longshore unions, construction unions and

electricians' unions) come within the scope of the proprietary definition used here. More broadly, stock and commodity exchanges
that permit the sale of seats may be usefully viewed as proprietary
unions. Members of the New York Stock Exchange,[26] for example,
lawfully fixed commission rates until recently, and still elect
managers of the exchange, pay fees and dues to maintain it, and
are allowed to sell their membership to *acceptable* would-be
brokers.[27]

Still another example of proprietary unions, broadly defined,
are the Pacific Northwest worker-owned plywood co-ops.[28] In these
organizations most workers are required to purchase at least one
share of ownership in the organization as a cost of entering employment. These shares are transferable to other would-be worker-
owners within reasonable limitations imposed by the respective
boards of directors.

Explicit proprietary arrangements existed at the turn of the
century. A Seattle longshore union issued negotiable stock certificates to its members. Each certificate represented a preferential
claim to work opportunity over noncertificated longshoremen. Any
claim holder had the right to sell it to the highest bidder.[29]
Proprietary-like activities have been observed among modern longshore unions where work assignments are allocated by seniority and
union claims on work opportunities at the docks. These claims are
transferable de facto and are rented by dock workers with less
valuable claims to work opportunities for short periods of time.[30]

For simplicity, let us assume that there are no limitations on the
number of memberships an individual worker may purchase and
hold, and that voting members monitor their leaders costlessly.
Assume also that divergent interests among members and between
members and leaders are nonexistent (i.e., preferences are identical). Although the costs of nonrent maximizing behavior, under
these institutional arrangements, are relatively higher than where
no proprietary interest is present, they do not necessarily imply the
rent-maximizing outcome. That is, the set of goods that equates
marginal utilities per dollar of expenditure for a given member can
be different from the set that would maximize aggregate rents for
him and his colleagues.[31] We may only say, a priori, that, given our
proprietary assumptions, choices that move the union away from
rent maximization for the collective are more costly for him than
choices that move him toward rent maximization. We will keep the

utility framework in this chapter to provide continuity when contrasting implications derived in the following sections with an analysis of the nonproprietary union in chapter five.

WAGE-MEMBERSHIP POLICY

In the case of the proprietary union, we have argued that bargaining goals will be consistent with, or at least be more likely to approximate, the maximization of rents. Associated with this level of rents is a unique quantity of labor services (man-hours) demanded by the employer(s). For simplicity, let us assume that all labor services are provided at a uniform cost, so that no price discrimination among employers exists. Holding total man-hours constant, what would be the optimal membership size of the union? Membership size will depend on the relationships between the cost of restricting entry into the trade or industry, the costs of rationing rent yielding jobs among new and incumbent members, the costs of transacting with new members, and the price (initiation fees and dues) of membership.

Benefits arising from collective bargaining are predominantly public and it should not be surprising that free-rider prospects might initially discourage many workers and would-be workers from becoming union members. Free riding, however, need not prohibit *all* collective action so long as there are at least some workers who would receive personal or individual benefits that were greater than the total cost of producing them. More formally, where the total gain to the group affected exceeds the total costs of providing the collective good, by more than it exceeds the gain to one or more individuals in the group, at least some of the collective good is likely to be produced.[32] Early organization of unions by relatively small groups of workers, possessing little institutionally derived coercive power vis-à-vis fellow employees and would-be employees, is not inconsistent with this hypothesis and explains how collective bargaining could be accomplished without universal membership or coercive action. Thus, it is not ad hoc or illegitimate to begin our analysis with the assumption that some subgroup of employees have voluntarily withheld their labor services in collective action in order to improve the terms of trade with their employer and produce economic rents for themselves as well as some nonmember-employees.

Of course, the success of this effort also rests with the wage elasticity of demand for the services of labor. The fruits of collective action will be greater the lower this demand elasticity is. Under certain conditions, lower demand elasticity is more likely where the resulting beneficiaries of collective action constitute a relatively small factor in the total cost of producing the final product.[33]

To further simplify the analysis that follows, either disregard, momentarily, nonpecuniary sources of rents or, alternatively, assume that all payment forms (pecuniary and nonpecuniary) can be expressed as a variable cost *per worker* and are acted upon as such by the firm(s). In figure 4.1, the union faces demand curve DD and marginal revenue curve MR. Curve SS is the labor supply

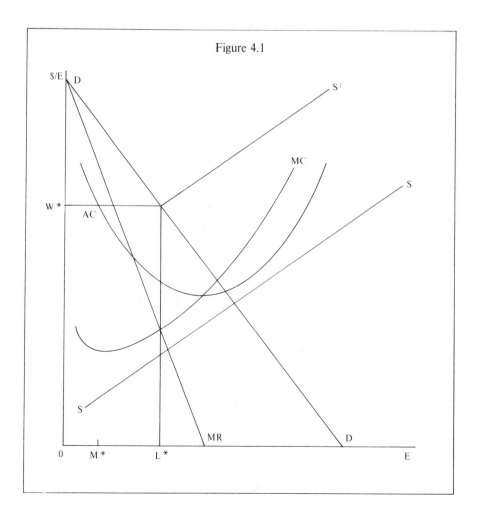

Figure 4.1

curve to the firm(s) and AC and MC are the union's average and marginal costs, including strike costs, collective bargaining costs, and the reservation prices of current and prospective members.[34] In the simple monopoly case, given hours per worker ($\bar{h}$), the rent-maximizing level of employment is L*. If initial membership were M*, the union would face several options. For example, it could seek to restrict labor market entry beyond L* and resign itself to share rents with L - M* *nonunion* workers at W*.[35] Since market entry restriction is not costless, union rents will be smaller by the increment in resource commitment that entry restriction requires. If we assume that these costs do not vary with employment or membership, this would be reflected in an upward shift in the AC curve in figure 4.1. Such entry restriction would have the effect of shifting SS beyond L* to S'.

A second option is to restrict entry still further so that even L* - M* nonmembers must expend all their expected rents just to find employment in the industry. Since this would leave them with no more than they could earn elsewhere, any potential rent dissipation by nonmembers would be effectively nullified. Rents per M* member may or may not be larger than before depending on the cost of these even more stringent restrictions (i.e., AC in fig. 4.1 would be shifted up even further and rents to workers may be smaller). To the extent that rents are in fact larger, this second option will be preferred to the first, although membership remains the same at M* in both cases.[36]

A third option consists of doing nothing to restrict entry into the labor market and opening up union rolls to all who wish to join at W*, subject to the constraint that long run costs to the organization must be covered. Since this would produce rent-dissipating competition for L* jobs, the union would seek to ration jobs by bargaining for limits to the hours an individual may work, and adopting other complementary criteria such as work assignment schemes by union membership or seniority.[37]

These schemes, in particular, have the virtue of diminishing member incentives to expend resources in an attempt to gain access to more of the available rent and thus serve to minimize rent dissipation itself. Moreover, increasing membership beyond M*, by opening up union roles, raises the prospect of extracting rents, via initiation fees, dues and wage differentials, that would otherwise be captured or dissipated by L* - M* nonmembers, in the second option. However, unlimited entry accompanied by rent-preserving, job-rationing criteria requires a resource commitment, on the part of unions, to monitoring and policing such mechanisms, and this is also costly. Still, it is certainly conceivable that the costs of entry restriction, associated with the first two options, can be so great that unlimited membership schemes would be rent-maximizing. This suggests that the rent maximizing model of a proprietary union is not limited to craft unions with closed shoplike arrangements such as referral halls.

Finally, unions face the option of committing resources to entry restriction beyond L* and *selling* memberships to L* - M* new members. To the extent that entry restriction is the least cost means of allocating rent-yielding jobs, and transaction costs are not prohibitive, this scheme has the virtue of avoiding rent dissipation arising from excess supply and of appropriating rents for the original M* members (otherwise appropriated or dissipated by L* - M* nonmembers) without extending membership beyond L*. In this scheme members can work as much as they want to at the W* rate.[38] This final option is a hybrid of options 1 and 3. It differs, however, from option 3 in an important way. In option 3, membership beyond M* might be adopted *even where rents could not be extracted from new members*. This is not so for our last alternative. That is, if entry restriction were *not* prohibitive (the converse of option three) but M* membership was prevented from sharing in rents acquired by members L* - M*, because transaction costs were prohibitive, then optimal membership would not exceed M*. This result is particularly important in understanding union wage-membership policy where there is a change in labor demand. This will be discussed more fully below.

The above discussion, by itself, however, yields few implications, since it merely describes conditions that effect membership size under assumptions of proprietary unionism and rent maximization. Nevertheless, two implications do suggest themselves. First, where entry restrictions exist, as in the case of occupational licensing and the closed shop, job assignment devices such as work rotation schemes, seniority job allocation and union preference rules should be absent.[39] Second, confiscatory wage policies based on membership attrition, in the face of stable demand, will be used only where incumbent members cannot appropriate or extract rents from replacements.[40]

AN INCREASE IN LABOR DEMAND

Further implications require the use of comparative statistics. For example, what might be a proprietary union's wage-membership policy in the face of an increase in labor demand? Assume that existing membership size is at L*(M*) in figure 4.2, and that the union is maximizing the present value of rents at uniform wage rates or labor costs per worker. A nontransitory rise in demand permits an increase in rents, given the cost of negotiation and strikes.[41] Our analysis suggests that proprietary unions can be expected to raise wage rates *and* allow employment and membership to expand. In figure 4.2 the union's bargaining goals, consistent with rent maximization, would warrant a wage and membership outcome of Ŵ, L̂(M̂) if entry restriction costs are not prohibitive. This

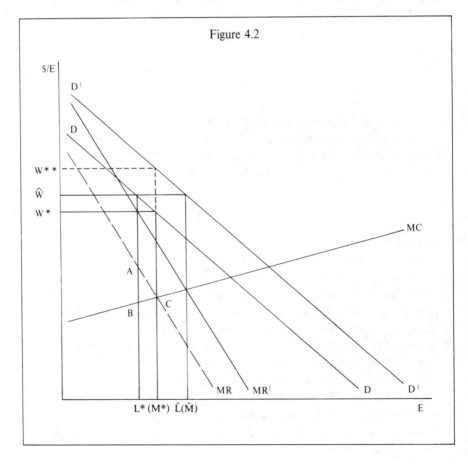

Figure 4.2

result is particularly interesting because it has been alleged to be *nonwealth-maximizing*. " . . .The typical union does not regard demand for more labor than the *current membership* can supply as evidence it has set the wage rate too low, as would an income maximizing union."[42] This statement implies that in an income-maximizing union, the wage rate in 4.2 should rise to W** and employment-membership, other things the same, should remain at L*(M*). Our analysis, on the other hand, suggests that even if the wage dimension of rents were the only one on which policy were to operate (as we have been assuming) the proprietary union, faced with nonprohibitive transaction costs, would find it wealth maximizing to expand employment-membership *so long as* the increments in rents were appropriable by incumbents.[43]

To the extent that increases in demand are expected to be "temporary," or transitory so that it would be too costly to bargain for higher wages, access rights to "temporary" rents at existing wage rates would be sold to would-be entrants and distributed among incumbents. Work permits constitute a real world expression of this type of transaction. Erroneous implications arise from a failure to recognize that the wage package need not be the only source of rents to incumbent owner-members in a proprietary union. New members are also a source of rents.

In terms of the utility-maximizing model discussed earlier, an increase in the demand for labor signals opportunities for incumbents to increase rents in both pecuniary and nonpecuniary form. To the extent that members view a change in general purchasing power resulting from union activity as a change in a *collective* benefit, the nominal price of this incremental benefit to any given member is zero; since his wage rate can be improved without reducing the wage rates for other members.[44]

If the given member-worker faces a zero nominal price for improving his command over general purchasing power, and *therefore* over the Hicksian composite good, G_o, that is purchased with money income, expression (4.6) becomes:

$$\frac{\theta \partial u / \partial g_j}{\theta \partial u / \partial G_o} = \frac{\varrho_j - \partial \varrho_m / \partial g_j}{- \partial \varrho_m / \partial G_o} \qquad (6')$$

An increase in labor demand raises ϱ_m, for all $\partial \varrho_m / \partial g_i > 0$, causing the effective prices of all rent-enhancing elements in the representative member's utility function to fall relative to the prices of nonrent affecting activities. Thus, an increase in labor demand will cause an increase in the quantity of rent-enhancing elements demanded by members. Two of these elements are wage rates and union memberships.

An increase in labor demand, as seen by the union member, raises (ϱ_m), thereby lowering the cost of generalized purchasing power (wages) relative to nonrent-enhancing activities. But a higher union wage demand is only one means for incumbents to capture the larger rents associated with an increase in labor demand. Another means, in a proprietary union, is through the sale of new memberships.[45] As labor demand increases, incumbents can capture some or all of the rents that would otherwise accrue to new workers by selling memberships to them at initiation fees or monthly dues, or by less direct methods such as establishing wage or dues differentials between newcomers and incumbents, that reflect the capital value of union generated rents. The less able are incumbents to capture these rents from new employees the less they are willing to accept wage increases that allow the firm to expand employment in response to an increase in labor demand. This analysis offers an appealing rationale for the inclusion of employment in the utility function of union members as discussed by Cartter (1959) and Atherton (1973).[46] Incumbent members are concerned about variations in employment that result from wage policy because changes in the employment of other workers affects the appropriation of rents.

A DECREASE IN DEMAND

Once new members have been admitted, what would be a proprietary union's policy in the face of a decrease in demand? A union "owned" by a single monopolist buying and reselling labor services at a uniform price would cut the wage to the new rent-maximizing level, since the owner can capture all of the remaining rents. In figure 4.2, choosing W* instead of Ŵ, at the new level of demand, means that the union will capture ABC rents.

Where ownership is divided among members who themselves feel the prospect of unemployment and the associated threat to their claim on any remaining future rents, wage-membership policy will depend on the probability distribution of layoffs, the transactions cost of pooling income among employed and unemployed members, and the cost of appropriating rents in addition to those that are directly appropriated from wage differentials. If each member had an equal chance of being laid off, and that chance were known, and if the costs of pooling income were not prohibitive, then members would choose the new rent-maximizing combination if they could agree to transfer some of these rents to members left unemployed. These transfers could take the forms of supplemental unemployment benefits, of subsidies to relocate, retrain or otherwise leave the industry, or of work sharing and featherbedding schemes. This implication, however, conflicts with the results of an expected utility model recently presented by Moore (1975), which he claims is "especially relevant to labor union behavior in deciding on wage cuts."[47]

Moore's model is simple and straightforward. Assume that the probability of a layoff, in response to a decline in demand, is known and identical for each worker-member. Then, if the utility of income earned, after a wage cut (guarantying continued employment), is less than the expected utility of the uncertain prospect (that a given worker will survive the layoff at the existing wage or be sacked at the income of his next best alternative), a rational individual member would vote to reject that wage cut. For certain parameter values, *all* workers would vote against a wage cut.[48] Although Moore's model assumes nothing about the objective function of a union, it implies that members of a wealth-maximizing union (in our model a proprietary union) would choose a nonrent-maximizing solution, questions of risk preference aside.

If transactions costs are nonprohibitive, Moore's implication must surely be wrong, because it ignores the rents that would be forsaken to the members, employed *and* laid off, if a wage cut were resisted. As long as pooling is permitted, there will be at least one distribution of remaining rents that would move *all* members to vote for a cut to the rent-maximizing wage.[49] Moreover, given costless pooling, no one will vote to cut the wage rate further.[50]

Moore's claims to the contrary, his analysis seems especially relevant to the *competitive* sector of the labor market. Given a reduced demand for labor, a refusal to cut wages under these conditions does not imply forsaken rents. Moore's conclusion, that his model applies to *both* unionized and nonunionized labor, is perhaps the result of treating unions as if they did not face a negatively sloped marginal revenue schedule.

When the assumptions of proprietary unionism and zero transactions cost are relaxed,[51] Moore's model does provide an interesting and plausible explanation for downwardly rigid wages in
unionized labor markets without introducing seniority institutions.

In terms of the utility analysis expresed in (6') above, the fall
in demand has reduced the level of rents and raised the effective
price of activities associated with enhancing rents such as demands
for higher wages. Thus, we can expect wage demands to fall relatively and absolutely. A fall in wage demands will actually salvage
more rent for incumbents than maintaining the old wage demand
or raising it. This follows because more members who will be generating at least some rent will be retained.

To continue with our proprietary model, assume that the distribution of layoff probabilities is skewed, as in the case where a
subset of the membership has seniority rights that assign to it lower
layoff probabilities at the expense of other members. So long as the
decline in demand does not threaten this subset at the existing
wage rate and as long as a majority of members will remain employed at the old rate, the membership will not vote for a wage
reduction that would maximize total rents. This result, however,
ignores two independent considerations. First, where those left
unemployed pose an imminent competitive threat to those remaining employed, a rent-maximizing wage cut will reduce that threat
and provide funds for supplemental unemployment benefits for
those who are still left unemployed. The second consideration is the
most relevant for our purposes. If incumbent union members also
share in the remaining rents salvaged by a wage cut, their total
wealth can be enhanced over and above that captured by resisting
any wage reduction.

PRICE LEVEL EFFECTS ON
PROPRIETARY UNION BEHAVIOR

There have been numerous inflationary periods where prices of
final goods and services have risen faster than wage rates.[52] The effect of a rise in the price level is to reduce the real value of money
wage income, wh/P^*, (both current and deferred) together with all
other fixed monetary claims relative to leisure. Since there are both
income and substitution effects associated with a reduction in real
earnings per hour, the consequences of this change on the supply of

union man-hours and on union wage demands is ambiguous. This is the conclusion reached by Atherton (1973), who then goes on, as discussed above, to customize union utility functions in order to resolve the ambiguity.[53] The effect of the unanticipated price level change on the supply of union resources employed in rent producing activities, however, is not ambiguous. Although Atherton does not attempt to present a theory of the determinants of his "strike length function,"[54] he assumes that the function remains unaltered when real wage income falls.[55] To the extent that strikes may yield rents, the fall in the real value of wage income has also reduced the cost of striking, i.e., has also reduced the forsaken real income associated with withholding services. It may be objected that the implication of increased strikes or strike length is a substitution effect of the reduction in real earnings, and will be offset by the accompanying income effect. But a strike may also be an investment in generating more income for members. To the extent that strikes can generate relatively more income than can continued work, a strike is also implied by an income effect. Thus, *both* the substitution and income effects of a reduction in real earnings, arising from a price level change, suggest the formation of bargaining policy that favors more or longer strikes to increase the nominal pecuniary portion of the remuneration package, and restore real rents.

A fall in the real value of wage income due to an increase in the price level will reduce consumption of goods purchased with money wages. Other things the same, the consumption of G_o should fall. But a rise in P* will also lower the real value of pecuniary rents, an element in the effective price of G_o See expression (6'). This is so because we have assumed that rents in general purchasing power form dominate ϱ_m, and wh/P* is contained in ϱ_m. A fall in ϱ_m, will reduce the effective price of G_o, in expression (6'), relative to the effective price of g_j, an element in G_1.[56] Ceteris paribus, the income compensated effect of this change in relative prices will be to favor higher rates of consumption of G_o to levels that obtained before the rise in P*. This may only be achieved by demanding higher money wage rates. Thus, union members respond to an increase in the price level, that lowers real wealth, by demanding wage increases that will restore real rents to their former levels. This same result is suggested by the utility-maximizing model presented above. If we separate utility affecting goods associated with union membership into those having the characteristics of collective goods (e.g., improved plant lighting) and those having the characteristics of private goods (e.g., the introduction of a lunchroom where employees buy food), we can use expression (6') to generate some more implications.

To the extent that an increase in income tax rates adversely affects workers relative to their employers, the cost of a strike to members falls relative to its cost to employers, and the same conclusions observed for price level changes apply. Union member demands for higher wage rates to restore the real value of pecuniary rents, reduced by higher taxes, would be expressed in collective bargaining goals.

The above analysis was based on the assumption of *unanticipated* inflation, a case that perhaps has been typical of a great deal of union experience.[57] If price level changes are *anticipated* by union members, even though the precise amount may be uncertain, we can no longer be confident that the attempts by the union to maintain real income levels will manifest themselves solely in terms of wage demands. Even escalator clauses provide only ex post facto protection. Therefore, economic theory suggests that anticipated inflation should also increase demands for remuneration *in kind*. This follows, because price level increases will erode the real value of these payments relatively less than they will erode wages and other pecuniary claims. "Free" goods supplied by the employer, such as lunches, commuter service, work clothes, housing, prepaid medical services, etc., are then relatively less costly than they would be if acquired by general purchasing power. Thus, anticipated inflation should cause unions to change the mix of bargaining goals they seek to achieve, relative to periods of stable prices, so that nonpecuniary elements receive relatively more weight.

HETEROGENEOUS PREFERENCES

We have so far studiously avoided one of the more interesting features of the trade union, the heterogeneity of preferences of the rank and file. We have been assuming identical preferences. Two related considerations, however, question the gravity of this "sin of omission." In the first place, different preference functions among union members are relevant where union procedure requires policy ratification by vote. Questions dealing with the ratification of bargaining agreements, changes in initiation fees, dues and other assessments, membership criteria, and union affiliation may be subject to majority vote. Thus, it would seem that obedient union managers need only take account of the preferences of the median voter. However, where the costs of transaction are not prohibitive, the median vote can be bought either indirectly via side payments or directly via the purchase and sale of incumbent job rights by other incumbents. As long as the median voter can be made at least as well off under rent maximization as he would have been if he were to pursue the maximization of his own utility independent of such compensation, the relevance of heterogeneous preferences in a theory of the proprietary union would be minimized.[58] Moreover, because job rights are transferable, they will be traded in the market like other assets and moved to their highest valued uses. Would-be members with tastes for bargaining packages more consistent with configurations of pecuniary and nonpecuniary elements that constitute maximum rents are more likely to directly bid ownership away from members with different preferences. It is not necessary that *all* nonrent maximizing tastes be bought out; it is only necessary that the number be sufficient to affect the median voter.

Once we recognize that side payments may be costly to effect, especially in unions with "large" memberships,[59] and that transactions in union cards may be prohibitively costly to consummate, the relevance of nonrent-maximizing tastes and heterogeneous preferences appear to loom larger. But the existence of such prohibitive costs questions the relevance of the proprietary assumption that access rights to rent-yielding jobs are exclusive and transferable.

In the next chapter proprietary assumptions are modified so that access rights to rent-yielding jobs are not transferable in the same way or degree as they have been in the paradigm just discussed. We continue to assume, however, that union leaders are costlessly monitored by their constituency and that their objectives are consistent with the interests of the median rank and file voter. These assumptions are relaxed in chapter six.

SUMMARY

Before moving on to the nonproprietary union, it will be useful to summarize the implications that have been derived from the proprietary model introduced in this chapter. Because members of a proprietary union may appropriate the capital value of rents derived from union activity, the wage and membership policies that they will support will be consistent with the maximization of monopoly rent. This hypothesis has suggested several implications. They are:

(a) Proprietary union wage policy will be positively correlated with nontransitory fluctuations in labor demand, so that union wage demands will be flexible (not rigid) and symmetrical.

(b) Proprietary unions will respond to nontransitory excess labor demands (supplies) by choosing a wage policy that permits both wage rates *and* employed membership to expand (contract) as a function of union demand and marginal cost elasticities.

(c) Proprietary unions will respond to unanticipated price level increases by increasing nominal wage demands to restore real rent levels.

(d) Anticipated price level increases will be associated with demands for escalator clauses and in-kind payments in lieu of some money wage payments in collective bargaining agreements.

(e) Proprietary unions will ration transitory increases in labor demands, at existing wage rates, by selling temporary work permits or by extracting "kickbacks," at market-clearing levels from temporary hires.

(f) Because monopoly rents may be appropriated by incumbents, proprietary union wage and membership policies should not produce membership or employment queues or waiting lists.

(g) Proprietary union wage policies will not be designed so that they threaten the survival of firms that are party to (or expected to be) the collective agreement.

5

The Nonproprietary Union

THERE are countless books and articles describing union institutions at all levels and across many separate organizations. These descriptions clearly establish that, except for some filial preference arrangements, the intent of unions has been to prohibit and penalize individual and unauthorized transfers of membership status by incumbents to would-be unionists.[1] Explicit private property in trade union membership exists only in the breach.[2]

Why haven't unions included the right to transfer title to memberships in the bundle of rights associated with membership status? At least two explanations suggest themselves. First, additional memberships in a union of nonhomogeneous workers increases the probability of pecuniary and nonpecuniary externalities. The physical characteristics, personality, religion and political convictions of the stockholder in a public corporation are less relevant to other owners than they would be to members of a trade union. The former do not work or socialize with each other; the latter usually do. If would-be unionists are capable of heaping pecuniary damages (e.g., by violating the "standard rate") or nonpecuniary damages (e.g., by presenting offensive personal characteristics to other members) on incumbents, these potential damages are viewed as collective or public. The price an individual incumbent member is willing to accept for his union card, or his right to membership, may be much less than the value of the total harm imposed on other members by the sale of that card. Before the other members would honor the rights attached to a transferred card, a majority of them would have to be compensated for any losses they anticipate as a result of the transfer. The cost of transacting such side payments, if they could be determined accurately (members would be prone to exaggerate damage), most likely would be prohibitive.

It may be objected that the same analysis is applicable to country club memberships. That is, the benefits of country club membership is significantly affected by the socioeconomic and personal characteristics of fellow members. Not all would-be members will enhance benefits for incumbents. The indiscriminate transfer of membership status between two private parties to the exclusion of the collective interest of the club may very well threaten that interest. Yet, unlike the practice in most trade unions, many country clubs include in the bundle of rights associated with membership, the right to transfer title to membership subject to the approval of other members or a board of governors. Would not the same arrangement be possible among trade unions? After all, ownership shares in worker-owned Pacific Northwest plywood co-ops and among members of the New York Stock Exchange are salable with the consent of monitoring bodies. Why not in trade unions?

Unlike social clubs, the New York Stock Exchange and plywood co-ops, the average size of national trade unions is relatively large. The larger the number of potential transactions, the higher the cost of monitoring to safeguard collective interests. Prohibiting the transfer of union cards may be oppressive to individual incumbent members but may be beneficial to the union as a collective. This interpretation is consistent with the observation that transferable membership rights are usually found among the smaller national unions. These are more often craft unions. Moreover, as in the case of other insitutions where membership rights are transferable, alienable membership rights in trade unions are also attenuated. To insure that the "right" type of people acquire membership rights from incumbents, transferability is limited to the immediate relatives of existing members. "Keeping it in the family," so to speak, economizes on the cost of information that is associated with investigating the characteristics of would-be applicants and screening new members.[3]

The above hypothesis does not fully explain the pervasive absence of private-property in union membership because it ignores the influence of employers. For example, if the employer has relatively little discretion in the hiring process, as in the case of hiring halls and other referral systems, and if a large variance in employee performance is relatively costly to the firm, the latter will not be indifferent to the characteristics of the employees referred to it. This suggests that any additional hiring costs imposed upon employers will be shifted back on to wage rates and thus affect the potential rents to all members of the union. Although transfer rights may be valuable to each individual member, their adoption may lower total rents below what they would be if cards were not transferable. Additionally, in a union shop situation, the purchase of a union card or some other evidence of membership rights, from a recent resignee, does not purchase access to employment. The buyer may be unacceptable to the employer as a replacement for the departing worker or as a new addition to the firm, at union scale wage rates. If transferability is subject to employer approval, employers with relatively large numbers of workers will attempt to shift the costs of monitoring and policing transactions on to union members through bureaucratic screening procedures. The effect of this may be to severely limit the value of transferability rights to members.[4]

Once it is recognized that job rights are costly to transfer, the cost of nonrent-maximizing behavior is lowered and the link between the maximization of rents and utility, as discussed in chapter four, is loosened for every union member. Without transferability, persons with preferences more consistent with rent maximization must incur higher costs to induce members with other preferences to pursue rent-maximizing behavior. Moreover, they have less incentive to do so if they themselves are handicapped in appropriating the full rents supplied by such actions. Therefore, in modeling union behavior it is important to be able to calibrate the degree of ownership enjoyed by union members.

THE OWNERSHIP INDEX

The choice theoretic structure for a given union member, as it relates to the objectives of union policy, was given by expression (6) in chapter four. Specification of the ownership characteristics of a given union should not affect the form or content of the utility function of any given member of that union. This suggests that expression (6) is applicable to both proprietary and nonproprietary union-member behavior. On the other hand, the ownership characteristics of a particular union are relevant to the form and content of the function that constrains utility affecting behavior in a given member. This suggests that the utility constraint as expressed in

(5.2), in chapter four, must be modified to account for the configuration of property rights among union members that characterizes ownership in a given organization. Let expression (5.2') represent the constraint on utility maximization in a *nonproprietary* union.

$$(P_oG_o)_m + (P_1G_1)_m \leqslant \alpha\varrho_m + (\hat{w}\hat{h}) + (P_1'G_1')_m + Y_m \qquad (5.2')$$

This is identical to expression (5.2) except for the addition of α. Let α be an index of ownership in the union that measures the fraction of a member's potential rents, in present value terms (ϱ_m), that he may actually appropriate in the current period.

Where a given individual may fully participate in any and all union generated rents immediately upon acquiring membership status, where he can transfer (for a consideration) the right to participate in union generated rents, and where the cost of enforcing his claim is nonprohibitive, the proprietary or ownership index α takes on the value of 1.[5] Under such conditions, the scarcity value of the union card is equal to the present value of the stream of rents a given owner can expect to appropriate over n periods, ceteris paribus. On the other hand, where rents are unassignable, or where enforcement costs are prohibitive and members may not even participate in rents as they occur at any moment in time, α has a value of zero; as has the scarcity value of a union card.[6] Between these two extreme values of α, lies a continuum of values reflecting numerous permutations and combinations of possible ownership configurations for union members. For example, between two unions that have virtually identical participatory rules for members in collectively generated monopoly rents, save for the fact that in one union incumbent members may bequeath their union cards to relatives while in the other union such transfers are prohibited, we can say that the value of α in the former is greater than in the latter. We can also say that the value of α in the former union is less than 1. For the purpose of the analysis that follows, we will assume that α is exogenous to the decision calculus of any given union member. This assumption shall be maintained throughout, since we are interested in the behavior of union members under different configurations of ownership rights, rather than how unions determine what ownership arrangements to adopt.[7]

The introduction of the exogenuous α factor into the utility-maximizing calculus of the union member, yields the following first-order condition in the g_jth good:

$$\frac{d\phi}{dg_j} = \frac{\theta \partial \upsilon}{\partial g_j} - \frac{\lambda[p_j - \alpha \partial \varrho_m]}{\partial g_j} = 0 \qquad (5.5')$$

From expression (5.5'), the effective price of a unit of the g_jth good is written $p_j - \alpha \partial \varrho_m / \partial g_j$. Between any two goods, g_i and g_j, utility is maximized for the individual union member where

$$\frac{\theta \partial \upsilon / g_i}{\theta \partial \upsilon / g_j} = \frac{p_i - \alpha \partial \varrho_m / \partial g_i}{p_j - \alpha \partial \varrho_m / \partial g_j} \qquad (7)$$

Except for the introduction of α, and the substitution of p_i and g_i for P_o and G_o, the above expression is similar to expression (6) in chapter four.[8] There, members held private-property rights in union cards and α was implicitly assumed to equal 1.

SOME GENERAL IMPLICATIONS

1. In the extreme case where $\alpha = 0$, so that no rents may be appropriated by members, the mix of goods for which members wish to bargain will not be influenced by any rent-enhancing opportunities associated with them. For example, assume in (7) that $\partial \varrho_m / \partial g_j > 0$ while $\partial \varrho_m / \partial g_i < 0$. Now compare *effective* relative prices between g_i and g_j where $\alpha = 0$ and $\alpha = 1$. In the latter case, the proprietary case, the ratio of effective prices favors the consumption of rent-enhancing goods g_j. In the extreme nonproprietary case, $\alpha = 0$, consumption is influenced by the ratio of market prices only, and the cost of *ignoring* rent-increasing possibilities is lowered.

2. Where job rights are nontransferable and only current rents are captured through pecuniary and non-pecuniary elements in the collective agreement, the value of α is greater than 0 but less than 1. To the extent that some policy choices, as expressed in the utility function of the median member-voter, yield more of their benefits in future periods, than other policy choices, the α assigned to the former will be smaller than the one assigned to the latter. Thus, in the nonproprietary case, as expressed in (7), the *effective price* of future oriented goals will be relatively higher than the price of present oriented goals and members will favor the latter.

3. Some elements in the individual member's utility function, that are also sources of rent, may have collective good characteristics. That is, any given member need not pay a rationing price to receive the benefits of such goods. Examples of goods with such characteristics include plant lighting, grievance procedures, and

wage rates. Other goods yielding utility to members, but for which a rationing price must be paid, include meals purchased by members in plant cafeterias, and pension and health programs to which members must contribute in order to receive matching employer contributions. In expression (7), let g_i be the collective good and g_j be a private good in the bargaining package for which the member must pay a transaction price, p_j. By comparison, members of unions having low α values will view private goods as relatively more expensive than collective goods. This follows because as α falls, the denominator in (7), the effective price of the private good, increases relative to the numerator, the effective price of the collective good whose transaction price, p_i, must be zero. Thus, we should expect these unions to place a relatively greater emphasis on collective good components in their bargaining packages than unions with higher α values.

The last two paragraphs suggest two more reasons why, in addition to the obvious benefits of general purchasing power in an exchange economy, nonproprietary unions usually emphasize wage increments relative to other rent sources in collective bargaining agreements. In the first place, increments in wage rates are sources of current consumption as opposed to future consumption.[9] In the second place, wage demands represent a collective good in the utility function of the individual member. A common response to higher wage demands, on the part of employers, is employment cutbacks through attrition. Since the great majority of collectively bargained wage increases occur in the absence of strikes and picketing,[10] it is not unreasonable to assume that individual union members behave as if the cost of a wage demand is zero.

Holding the price level and hours of work constant, demands for increased wage rates translate into demands for more G_o goods. Recall from chapter four that G_o is the vector of goods individual members may purchase in the market with their wages. Under the above assumptions, we may treat G_o as a Hicksian composite, *collective*, good. Expression (6') from chapter four may be rewritten as:

$$\frac{\theta \partial u / \partial G_o}{\theta \partial u / \partial g_j} = \frac{- \alpha \partial \varrho_m / \partial G_o}{p_j - \alpha \partial \varrho_m / \partial g_j} \tag{7'}$$

As the value of α is lowered, for a given union, members will view wage rate demands as a relatively less expensive source of utility compared with private good elements in the bargaining package. From the nonproprietary model we derive the following implication: unions with more nonproprietary characteristics, other things the same, should exhibit relatively greater interests in the wage rate, as a component of the bargaining package, than unions with relatively more proprietary characteristics.

Some evidence consistent with the above implication is available from the construction trades. A few years after the 1964 Civil Rights Act, the Department of Labor began to put pressure on referral unions (i.e., those unions that were the main source of labor supply to employers of union labor in their respective industries) to abandon their practice of selecting new members from among the sons and relatives of incumbents. These filial arrangements were said to promote the transfer of job rights in a racially biased manner. Incumbent union members enjoyed the right to transfer property in membership to offspring and other relatives. Abolition of that right effectively reduced the α value associated with future rents the union may generate for its members. One result of the decline in α, for these unions, was a rise in average wages for journeymen-building trade workers by 34.1 percent between 1968 and 1971, causing a decline thereafter in the market share of *unionized* construction firms.[11] Interestingly, average wage rates of union workers in durable goods manufacturing, populated by nonreferral unions that have never had proprietary rights in membership, rose by 18.1 percent during the same period.[12]

4. Finally, because membership is not transferable, the identification of collective bargaining objectives, in a nonproprietary union, will tend to ignore the more general interests of unknown would-be members and reflect relatively more of the idiosyncrasies of the existing membership. This follows because the cost of ignoring features that would make the union appealing to would-be members is relatively low in nonproprietary unions. Incumbent members cannot capture the capitalized value of the benefits that would accrue to new members attracted to the union.

To the extent that unionists are not identical, median voter preferences across unions need not be identical, and the components of bargaining packages of different nonproprietary unions within the same industry, or of different unions across industries, should evidence relatively wider variation when compared with the bargaining packages of proprietary unions. Comparisons between nonproprietary unions and nonunion situations should yield similar evidence. Although preferences for bargaining package components may vary among would-be proprietary unionists as well, incumbents of proprietary unions will incorporate some of the more obvious and common interests of would-be members into their bargaining demands. Since knowledge of these more obvious and common interests are available to all unions within an industry or to all unions across industries, it would not be surprising to find a narrower dispersion of bargaining package components among proprietary unions as they attempt to attract would-be members *at the margin*. The same analysis applies to nonunion situations. There, the discipline of the market forces employers, in the same industry, to compete for workers from a pool of individuals with varying tastes for wages, working conditions, and benefits. To be competitive, employers will offer those wage rates, working conditions and benefits that they perceive are most common and obvious and reflect would-be worker interests *at the margin*. Consequently, the dispersion of remuneration packages across nonunionized firms in the same industry should be narrower than the dispersion of remuneration packages (bargaining package components) among firms organized by nonproprietary unions in the same industry.

For example, the ratio of wage to nonwage benefits (in dollar terms) should exhibit a statistically significant variation across nonproprietary unions within the same industry or across industries, ceteris paribus. On the other hand, the ratio of wage to nonwage benefits (in dollar terms) under proprietary unionism should exhibit little or no significant variation across unions within the same industry or related industries. Some evidence consistent with this implication was reported by Solnick and Staller.[13] The authors use an industry-by-industry approach to estimate the impact of unionization on fringe benefit expenditures by employers. Their model is based on the assumption that employees pay for employer fringe benefit expenditures through foregone wage increases. Fringe benefits are confined to employer contributions to insurance plans and pension plans. A sample of 1,388 establishments was taken from the manufacturing sector. Approximately 68 percent of these establishments were unionized. Since most unions in this sector are not referral unions, there is a relatively high probability that they may be identified as having relatively low α values. Solnick and Staller found that unionization is associated with a 21 percent higher level of pension expenditures and a 38 percent higher level of insurance expenditures among manufacturing establishments once income, firm size, and regional variables were accounted for. However, an industry-by-industry comparison revealed relatively wide variation in these statistics. The authors found an explanation for this variation difficult to provide. According to Solnick and Staller:

> What we have not been able to do is to uncover the factors that explain the variance in union impact across industries. Since benefit expenditures have been negotiated over a period of years the use of cross-section data necessarily misses the historical development of compensation packages. The variance in union impact may result from differences in union strength, *differences in tastes among the workers or the union officials*, or differences in these factors over a number of years.[14]

CHANGES IN DEMAND AND UNION WAGE-EMPLOYMENT-MEMBERSHIP POLICY

As was discussed in chapter four, increases in labor demands signal opportunities to incumbents to increase rents in both pecuniary and nonpecuniary forms. Returning to expression (7), this suggests that the effective prices of all rent-enhancing (rent-inhibiting) elements in each member's utility function are lowered (raised), though not proportionally, relative to their levels before the change and relative to nonrent effecting goods.

$$\frac{\theta \partial u/g_i}{\theta \partial u/g_j} = \frac{p_i - \alpha \partial \varrho_m / \partial g_i}{P_j - \alpha \partial \varrho_m / \partial g_j} \tag{7}$$

If we assume that $\partial \varrho_m / \partial g_i > 0$ and that $\partial \varrho_m / \partial g_j < 0$, and if we further assume that $\alpha = 1$, then an increase in labor demand will lower the effective price in the numerator relative to the denominator and more of the rent-enhancing activity will be pursued by the membership. In this example, the case of a proprietary union, the increase in demand implies an expansion in membership at the expense of the maximum wage increment consistent with an employment level limited to the incumbent members.[15] This follows because it will be relatively more expensive for incumbent members to raise wage rates to the exclusion of any employment expansion.

The nonproprietary case permits no such conclusion. That is, if rents may not be appropriated from new members or if only a "small" fraction may be so appropriated (i.e., $\alpha < 1$), the effective price of expanding membership, as a device to increase rents and therefore utility, will *rise* relative to the effective price of other sources of utility associated with no increase in membership. One such source is the increment in general purchasing power implied by the wage increase that would limit employment to the existing membership.

Figure 5.1 shows this result more clearly. Assume incumbent members (m) face labor demand (DD) and marginal revenue (MR). The union's marginal costs of performing collective bargaining services, policing agreements and other such tasks for varying numbers of members and would-be members, is given by MC. This curve includes the reservation prices and opportunity cost of

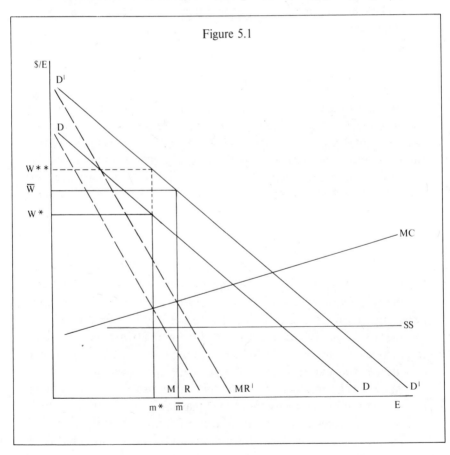

Figure 5.1

alternative numbers of incumbent and would-be members. Their supply function is shown by SS. For simplicity of exposition, the analysis abstracts from all nonpecuniary sources of rent. Membership size, at any given wage rate, is taken to equal total employment in the unionized firm or industry at that wage rate. At wage rate W*, rents are maximized and membership-employment is m*. This is the outcome expected if incumbents have full proprietary interests in membership, i.e., $\alpha = 1$. Now compare the results of a shift in demand on the wage-employment-membership policies of a union that has changed from proprietary to nonproprietary status. An example of such a change might be one where incumbent members of referral unions were prohibited from bequeathing their membership cards to offspring and other relatives, as discussed above.

If demand were increased to D'D', incumbents would be able to increase their share of rents up to some maximum. Under existing assumptions, the largest rent increment possible is that associated with a wage rate W̄ and a membership-employment level m̄. Since members of a proprietary union would be able to appropriate all of this increment through participation in the proceeds from the sale of new memberships—or in the case of a temporary increase in demand, through participation in the proceeds from the sale of work permits—they would support an increase in employment to m̄. For similar reasons, a decline in demand would not generate resistance to wage cuts by incumbent members. As long as incumbents may appropriate rent from newer members, it will pay the former to adopt wage policies that minimize the loss in aggregate rent and foster the continued employment of the latter group.[16]

Now assume that ownership rights in union membership status have been severely attenuated. Under nonproprietary conditions, participation in rent increments from the sale of new memberships is greatly curtailed. The returns to incumbent members from a wage policy that permitted expansion of membership-employment beyond existing levels would be smaller than would obtain by setting a wage at W** and limiting employment to m*.[17] This suggests that it is the nonproprietary, nonwealth maximizing union model rather than the proprietary model that predicts employment-inhibiting wage increases in response to increasing labor demand. This prediction, however, appears to be rejected by experience.[18]

In response to increases in labor demand, unions appear to pursue policies of wage *and* employment expansion. At least two complementary explanations, consistent with the nonproprietary model, suggest themselves. The first is that *some* employment expansion will be permitted if it is less costly to adopt pecuniary and nonpecuniary differentials between new and incumbent members as a means of extracting *current* rent, than to attempt a wage increase large enough to completely inhibit employment expansion. Journeymen-apprentice wage differentials, seniority wage and hours differentials, and deductions from current wage payments due new workers to support pension benefits for older workers nearing retirement, are other forms of current rent extraction and transfer to more tenured members.[19] Finally, transfers from newer to older members may also be achieved through overt and/or covert dues differentials.[20] These institutions provide a means for incumbents to participate in rents arising from employment expansion, thus raising the cost to existing members of ignoring this option when demand increases.[21] However, *future* wage differentials, given a "low" α, will be discounted more heavily than otherwise, and it is not expected that membership-employment will be expanded to the fully appropriable rent maximizing level ($\tilde{m}$).

The second explanation for membership-employment expansion focuses on the discretionary role of union managers.[22] There are several factors that encourage union managers, in the face of increased demand for labor, to bargain for wage rates and other remuneration that have the effect of expanding employment and membership beyond existing levels. Managers of most unions receive salaries that, in part, are positively associated with the membership size of the unions they administer and the value of organizational assets.[23] Since the initiation fees and dues of most unions are either fixed by constitution or subject to change only at the will of a majority of members,[24] managers have an incentive to expand membership, as a source of direct and indirect wealth for themselves. "Large" memberships and "large" treasuries, used to finance expense accounts and to purchase assets, should be sought by leaders at the expense of higher wage rates for incumbents and therefore smaller potential memberships. The sacrifice of rents, otherwise captured by incumbents, does not directly affect managers at the margin, because they do not directly share in them. This suggests that even if the salaries of managers did vary directly with the rents obtained by rank and file members, the former would still find it attractive—at the margin—to trade *some* of this reward for both "somewhat" higher executive salaries associated with larger memberships *and* for the nontaxable benefits associated with control over larger treasuries, expense accounts and trust funds.[25]

A DECREASE IN DEMAND

What would be the effect of a subsequent, nontransitory fall in labor demand on nonproprietary union policy goals? If demand subsequently and unexpectedly declines, so that employment for at least some members is threatened at the existing levels of remuneration, the effect of this would be to reduce the probability of retaining employment for *all* members below the probability that would have existed if employment and, therefore, membership had not been permitted to expand in the first place. As demand falls, rents at existing remuneration levels become negative and the effective price of maintaining or pursuing such policies increases. Note that from expression (7') negative rents will raise the effective price of collective goods relatively more than noncollective goods. Thus, one policy variable that might be expected to change is the wage rate. Incumbent members, however, will see a cut in wage rates as a transfer of wealth from themselves to the most recent additions to the organization, since any rents that may be saved by such an action will go to the latter members rather than the former. One way for older members to insulate themselves from such pressure, short of prohibiting expansion in the first place, is to assign different tenure probabilities to incumbents and to newcomers. Such insulation would allow newer members to bear the brunt of a reduction in rents due to a decline in labor demand.

Resistance to wage cuts, however, does not require preferential treatment for incumbents. As Moore has shown us,[26] even if the probability of layoff, in response to a decline in demand, is known and identical for each worker-member, a rational individual might vote to reject a wage cut. Such a decision will compare the utility of income earned after a wage cut, guarantying continued employment, and the expected utility of the uncertain prospect that a given worker will survive the layoff at the existing wage or be sacked at the income of his next best alternative. Moore shows us that, for certain parameter values, the union might experience a *unanimous* vote against a wage cut.[27] Of course few unions provide no insulation for incumbent members in facing a decline in demand. Many collective contracts have specified layoff criteria in terms of seniority systems and union classification.[28]

These comments suggest that the response of nonproprietary unions to reductions in demand will be less flexible than the response of proprietary unions. In the latter case incumbents would agree to wage reductions because they would participate in some of the income that newer members would be able to earn if allowed to retain their jobs. In the nonproprietary case, on the other hand, the cost of such participation is assumed to be higher or prohibitive, and the incentive to adopt a flexible wage policy is considerably lessened. Thus, although seniority-layoff criteria and other such schemes, intended to influence favorably the probability of continued employment among incumbent members, are implied by both proprietary and nonproprietary ownership arrangements, wage or remuneration flexibility is not. More specifically, the assumptions of the proprietary model unambiguously predict wage and employment symmetry in response to demand fluctuations. Although the wage and employment responses to an increase in demand are less clear under nonproprietary unionism, the model does suggest wage inflexibility in response to a decrease in labor demand.

PRICE LEVEL EFFECTS ON UNION WAGE POLICY

The analysis in chapter four, concerning price level effects on proprietary union bargaining goals, revealed that when the real value of rents declined, the relative costs of collective action (in terms of forsaken income) would also decline, making it economical to restore real income through demands for higher money wage rates and other sources of rents. In terms of expression (6′) in chapter four, the fall in the real value of rents due to a price level change lowered the effective price of collective relative to private good sources of utility to union members. Since a wage increase represents a collective source of utility to union members, the analysis suggested that union members would find it relatively less costly to restore real income through wage demands. This result obtained whether the declines in real rents were *unanticipated* (and therefore a catchup wage policy was sought) or *anticipated*, suggesting demands for escalator clauses and for a larger fraction of *real* collective goods in the bargaining package. If the full proprietary assumptions are relaxed, differences arise in union bargaining policy toward the composition of remuneration packages.

The nonproprietary case suggests that collective goods policy in general, and wage policy in particular, are likely to be less demanding in response to a rise in the price level than in the proprietary case. This follows because $\alpha < 1$ and the effective price of collective goods relative to private goods does not fall as much in the nonproprietary union with a given decline in real rents. For example, if $\alpha = .50$, a 5 percent rise in the cost of living that reduces the real value of rents proportionately[29] translates into a 2.5 percent fall in ϱ_m for both numerator and denominator in expression $(7')$.[30] Thus, the magnitude of demands for higher money wage rates and other collective goods relative to "private" goods, in response to a rise in the cost of living, will be smaller, the smaller α is.

If inflation is anticipated by union members, it will be discounted only imperfectly, since both future benefits and costs are not fully capitalized into the present in a nonproprietary union. This suggests that such unions will be less effective than would proprietary unions in insulating themselves from expected inflation. For example, unions with relatively low α values would be less likely to adopt escalator clauses in their bargaining policies.[31] Moreover, unions with relatively low α values will exhibit, in their current policy demands, smaller ratios of real to monetary remuneration than unions with relatively high α values. This is because the effective prices of nonpecuniary sources of rents will not fall as much in unions where changes in the future value of money income are only dimly perceived in the present.

Nevertheless, we may conclude that, although the magnitude may be relatively modest, the effect of an increase in the cost of living on nonproprietary unions is directionally the same as its effect on proprietary unions. A disproportionate increase in the price level will move unions to increase their money wage demands and their "willingness" to strike. Where inflations are anticipated, unions will attempt to insulate themselves against the higher cost of living by bargaining for anticipatory wage hikes, escalator clauses and a shift in the mix of elements in the remuneration package from general purchasing power to in-kind (real) sources of rents.

OWNERSHIP AND THE STRIKE PHENOMENON

Strikes, like negotiations, are costs of producing rents. If unions knew the bargaining package that employers would accept after a strike of some given length, and employers knew the package unions would accept after the same strike, both groups could gain by avoiding the costly contest and settling; provided that the minimum union demand was less than the maximum employer offer. The same may be said for the resources both sides expend in lengthy negotiations. But the production of information or knowledge is not costless. As a result, parties to negotiations can have different subjective estimates concerning the outcome of a strike, and this may be an important element in explaining why strikes are observed.[32] Just why strikes occur, however, is still a mystery that has eluded economic analysis. Nevertheless, we may be certain that a union's bargaining objectives are constrained by negotiation and strike costs. At this point, it is useful to remind the reader that it is not the purpose of this section, nor the purpose of this book, to develop a model of collective bargaining or of the decision to strike.[33] Rather, it is our intention to examine the influence that ownership characteristics have on the union strike phenomenon, ceteris paribus.

In one dimension, higher wage rate demands by unions will eventually meet with employer resistance. In multidimensional terms, the more valuable the remuneration package demanded by the union, the more resistant the firm will be beyond some level. As discussed earlier, firms will be less resistant to the components of some bargaining packages than to others of equal market value, if the firms have a comparative advantage in meeting the demands inherent in the former relative to the latter.

For members of nonproprietary unions, bargaining packages that threaten relatively greater employer resistance, and thus lower rents, may not be as forbidding as they might be to members of a proprietary union. This is because the cost to individual members in depleting current strike benefit funds (i.e., future assessments[34] against *future* wage earnings to replenish those funds) are not capitalized into the present value of membership status. Strikes and strike lengths that appear irrational to outside observers, because the increments won are equal to (or less than) the total costs of the strike, may be perfectly logical if a relatively larger fraction of benefits won are captured currently while a relatively larger fraction of costs are amortized over a longer period.[35] The incentives to ignore the costs of uneconomical strikes are so obvious that most unions are subject to a formal, two-stage *authorization* requirement, first by the leadership of the local union and then by the executive board of a national or international union. Penalties for ignoring this requirement include the withholding of strike funds by the international organization.[36]

In their hypothesis explaining the existence of strikes, Ashenfelter and Johnson portray the role of the union leader as "(doing) more than merely represent(ing) the wishes of the rank and file."[37] If the rank and file's expectations about achievable wage increases are much greater than the leaders', the latter will attempt to convince the membership to accept the smaller increase. This may be done with or without a strike. The former, however, has the effect of raising rank and file estimates of employer resistance to higher wage demands. Rather than sign an agreement for a lower wage increment and risk political backlash, the leadership is said to favor and *promote* a strike call.[38]

Ashenfelter and Johnson failed to explain why rank and file members resist the advice of their leadership. In their analysis, they assume a certain expertise among leaders and claim that "the leadership is aware of the possibilities of each bargaining situation . . . ."[39] They approvingly cite the experience of federal mediators who claim " . . . in many situations . . . (where) the union membership is unwilling to accept the reasonably attainable result of negotiations and is more militant than responsible leadership, a strike may be necessary to drive home the 'facts of life.' "[40] Why the apparent "unreasonableness" on the part of the rank and file, even in the face of more knowledgeable and presumably trustworthy sources? The answer is implied by our nonproprietary model.

"Unreasonable" and "irresponsible" rank and file demands are in fact rational for incumbent members, if the effective cost of realizing those demands is relatively low. Although wage rates and other demands for remuneration may be modified following the initiation of a strike, so will the offers of employers. The *estimated* returns to incumbent members, or to a majority of them, may be larger rather than smaller as a result of a strike, if the structure of rights to future benefits, and the structure of liabilities to future costs, are clearly recognized.

An analysis of the propensity to strike does not require a distinction between rank and file interests and leadership interests, as claimed by the Ashenfelter-Johnson hypothesis, although our analysis of nonproprietary unions implies such a distinction and suggests different conclusions.[41] The implication that derives from our analysis, and that distinguishes it from the A/J strike model, is that unions with higher α values will exhibit relatively fewer uneconomical strikes (and strikes that are of longer duration than the average length of strikes for all unions) than will unions identified as relatively nonproprietary (i.e., lower α values), ceteris paribus.

SUMMARY

The single most important characteristic of the nonproprietary model, that distinguishes it from the model of chapter four, is the relatively lower opportunity cost of nonrent maximizing behavior that is implied by less than full private property in union membership. This nonrent maximizing hypothesis generates several implications consistent with utility maximization for the median voter member, and, therefore, for union policy. They are:

(a) In response to an increase (decrease) in labor demand, changes in employed union membership (wage rates) should be relatively "rigid" or inflexible, when compared to corresponding changes in wage rates (employed union membership).

(b) Since nonproprietary unions are not expected to maximize monopoly rents, unanticipated inflations that reduce real rents are *not* expected to trigger demands for higher money wage rates that would fully restore these rents.

(c) The nonproprietary factor will dull relative price distinctions between future nominal and real elements in the bargaining package. This suggests that nonproprietary unions, in the face of anticipated inflations, will exhibit few significant differences in the composition of the bargaining packages (e.g., money wages vs. in-kind payments) demanded relative to bargaining packages demanded under stable prices.

(d) Because future vs. present distinctions are less clear in nonproprietary unions, escalator clauses and other such measures will be of limited use in the face of anticipated inflations.

(e) Collective bargaining policies formulated in nonproprietary unions will focus on the preferences of the median voter, rather than on the union member at the margin. To the extent that median voter preferences differ across unions in the same industry, components of bargaining packages (e.g., wage and nonwage elements) will evidence relatively wider variation when compared with remuneration packages across nonunionized firms in the same industry.

(f) Nonproprietary unions should have relatively more elaborate or restrictive strike-authorization procedures, relative to proprietary-like unions, to discourage uneconomic and excessive use of the strike.

(g) Unions with higher α values, i.e., unions with more proprietary features, will be less likely to engage in unauthorized, or "wildcat strikes," than will unions identified as relatively nonproprietary (i.e., lower α values).

(h) Unions with higher α values, proprietary features, will be less likely to run uneconomical strikes than will unions identified as relatively nonproprietary. One proxy for this phenomenon is the fraction of strikes of *longer than average duration* (compared to all unions) experienced by unions with nonproprietary features.

6

Managerial Discretion Within The Union

A LABOR union, like a publicly held corporation, owes much of its success to its ability in attracting large numbers of "investor-members" who are willing to commit resources to the formation, maintenance, and goal achievements of the organization. These resources may take the forms of initiation fees and dues assessments as well as foregone income resulting from strike and picketing activities. In an important sense these contributions constitute investments, similar to the purchase of equity shares in a corporation, that are expected to yield a net return in the form of positive wage and nonwage differentials in labor markets.[1] Since the magnitude of this return (net of member resource commitments) is not fixed, members may be viewed as residual claimants, the counterparts of corporate shareholders.[2] Abstracting momentarily from obvious ownership differences, both institutions face a common problem. If residual claims are distributed among large numbers of people, the gains or losses arising from unexpectedly good or bad decisionmaking are widely dispersed, and each *individual* member (shareholder) has the incentive to *shirk* in the collective production of net returns. This assumes an esoteric relationship between rents (profits) and *individual* productivity so that it is costly to discover productivity differences among members by examining final products.[3] Conversely, the fewer are the residual claimants and the closer are individuals' productivity correlated with final outcomes, the smaller is the incentive to engage in shirking.

Even if it were costless to police employer performance in executing the provisions of collective agreements[4], and even if participatory democracy within unions was so inexpensive to administer that each and every member voted on each and every union decision, the analysis so far suggests that it would be in the interests of most members to transfer decisionmaking authority to a smaller group (managers) whose main functions would be to monitor or police the rent producing activities of members and the integrity of the collective contract with the firm.[5] Union managers may or may not hold residual claims. The important point is that the potential for widespread shirking inherent in diffuse ownership arrangements generates a demand for monitoring services. Union management, empowered with disciplinary weapons such as the power of expulsion, provides monitoring services by locating, exposing and acting against shirkers on behalf of the residual claiming membership. But if union managers monitor the behavior of rank and file, who monitors the monitors?

Stockholders of private property corporations, instead of devoting resources to the monitoring and policing of management's decisions (more costly with many stockholders than with only a few), can exercise the right to sell ownership claims. This provides a lower-cost alternative for each stockholder than seeking to alter disagreeable decisions.[6] Moreover, "the policing of managerial shirking relies on across-market competition from new groups of would-be managers as well as competition from workers within the firm who seek to displace existing management."[7] A proprietary union would be able to offer similar safeguards. Members dissatisfied with the performance or policies of management would be able to withdraw their investment through the sale of union cards. Of course, this would constitute a costlier response than in the case of stockholders, since it would most likely mean changing jobs as well. But managerial shirking would be policed by interunion and intraunion competition for managerial positions.

Union managers are elected or appointed by the membership, not only because they provide an economical control over rank and file shirking, but also because they provide other services. Information about collective bargaining opportunities is costly to acquire and interpret, negotiations and planning are subject to economies of specialization, and the policing of collective bargaining agreements uses up resources. Managerial functions include the formulation of collective bargaining goals, the negotiation and monitoring of collective bargaining agreements, the policing of jurisdictional boundaries, and the administration of internal union affairs. The latter include disciplinary actions against members who threaten the monopoly position of the organization, adjudicating differences among members, and husbanding strike, pension and legal defense funds as well as general revenues. Union managers also perform valuable services in expediting and advocating the grievances of members and in administering and protecting seniority rights.

The effective conduct of these tasks often requires the sort of managerial discretion that is characteristic of the powers assigned to corporate executives. In general, it would be prohibitively costly to subject each and every problem or issue that confronts the union to popular discussion and vote. As a consequence, leaders are assigned or, by default, adopt for themselves, decisionmaking powers that could be used to improve the welfare of the membership. However, the costs of detecting managerial shirking and of enforcing contracts with leaders are all positive.

Other things the same, the policing policy that will maximize utility for members equates the marginal cost of detecting deviant behavior, and controlling it, with the marginal returns from such policies. This suggests that there will exist a range of managerial discretion in union affairs where leaders may deviate from the interests of the rank and file. The magnitude of this range will depend upon such things as the opportunities for, and the existence of rival unions, and of internal opposition, the costs of switching affiliation, the existence of *no raiding agreements* among unions, the geographic decentralization of the membership, the heterogeneity of member preferences, the total value of attainable rents, and the ownership characteristics of the union.[8]

MANAGERIAL CONSTRAINTS
IN A NONPROPRIETARY UNION

Two distinguishing features of nonproprietary unions are the nontransferability of membership rights and the absence of *personalized claims* to revenues deposited in union treasuries. These features bear heavily on the control of managerial discretion.

Nontransferability of membership rights precludes two sources of control or influence over managerial behavior that are available to stockholders in proprietary firms. First, members may not withdraw the capitalized values of the rent stream expected from their investments in response to undesirable managerial policies. Second, members cannot concentrate voting power in a few individuals for the purpose of changing managerial personnel.[9]

More importantly, however, the limited nature of an individual member's claim to rents (whether pecuniary or otherwise) and the collective nature of the gains arising from monitoring errant management, lower the returns to rank and file members of participating in efforts to detect, police, and change management. As a result, the nonproprietary character of most unions provides greater opportunities for managers or leaders, if they so choose, to increase their own utility "at the expense" of rank and file members. This suggests that rumors and accusations, as well as accurate information about poor union management, should instigate relatively little activity by rank and file members to reform such unions. "I got mine, why shouldn't he get his?"[10] is a philosophy that reflects the *free rider* implications of nonprivate property rights in union monopoly rents.

It also suggests that rank and file "apathy" on collective choice issues will dampen the flow of reform candidates challenging incumbents for power. Still, leaders will anticipate competition for their jobs as long as holding a leadership office permits a significant degree of discretionary behavior[11] (i.e., behavior inconsistent with dominant rank and file interests). Officers would be willing to expend some of the rents implied by exercise of that discretion to secure their tenure in the management of the union. This implication is consistent with the control union leaders have been observed to exercise over their union's information disseminating channels, making it difficult for potential opposition candidates to attract the attention of the membership. Constitutional clauses outlawing "dual unionism"[12] have been frequently used to silence opposition candidates and dissidents, as has the vague clause "conduct threatening to the security of the union."[13] Presidential powers to appoint committee members and fill staff positions have often provided the means to buy off opposition.[14] Finally, many national unions have failed to hold regular conventions and many locals have failed to hold regular meetings in attempts to avoid political confrontation.[15]

These considerations lead us to expect that the tenure of officials in nonproprietary unions should be longer, and the frequency of contested elections fewer, than experienced in proprietary organizations (both unions and corporations) of similar size[16] that elect their officers by shareholder or member vote. Moreover, among nonproprietary unions, the tenure of officials should be longer and contested elections fewer where union leaders have more managerial discretion than where they do not.

The above discussion is not meant to suggest that union management is unfettered by its membership and has full discretion over union policy decisions. Rather, it is meant to convey the notion that the structure of rights in labor unions yields logically refutable implications concerning the incentives "owner-members" will have to detect, police, and censure management discretion competitive with rank and file interests. Unless every policy decision is subject to membership ratification, managerial discretion will be a part of union institutional life.

For each rank and file member, however, there is some nominal level of utility, associated with alternative union policy choices, below which it is worthwhile to join with other members and threaten the political survival of incumbent officials.[17] This critical level represents a survival constraint on managerial behavior and in a heterogeneous union is associated with the median voter. Its height is a function of the existence of rival unions, the costs of forming and maintaining internal opposition to current leadership, the costs of changing over from one union to another, the existence and enforcement of no raiding agreements, and the personal benefits from changing administrations, which themselves are a function of the structure of rights facing members. Given a rival union and zero costs of monitoring and policing union leaders, the critical level of utility for the median voter would be identical to the maximum level attainable consistent with his wealth constraint. This analysis suggests that variations in the determinants of critical utility levels across unions should yield differences in the degree of managerial discretion exercised by union leaders.

To the extent that members anticipate excessive discretionary behavior on the part of management, it may be in their collective interest to devise bureaucratic procedures, rules, and requirements designed to constrain such discretion and reduce "mismanagement." For example, we would expect managerial decisions in unions to be subject to more frequent referendums than managerial decisions in publicly held corporations of similar size, as measured by voting shares outstanding. Decisions relating to the specification of wage rates and of working conditions negotiated in collective agreements, to strike calls, job actions, and slowdowns, to the purchase of assets and the issuances of indebtedness, and to the admittance of new members, are not infrequently subject to the vote of the membership or of convention delegates.[18] On the other hand, decisions relating to the pricing of products, to their quality and level of production, to the issuance of indebtedness, and to the sale of additional stock certificates are rarely, if ever, subject to referendum in publicly held corporations.

The implication that is suggested by such rules is that the asset structure of nonproprietary unions will appear relatively more conservative when compared with the investment policies of proprietary organizations, including corporations. For example, compare pension fund investments wholly managed by a nonproprietary union with pension fund investments of ununionized proprietary corporations.[19]

The absence or attentuation, in nonproprietary unions, of a single all-encompassing criterion, such as the maximization of union monopoly rent, implies a greater variety of bureaucratic constraints on leaders than would be observed under proprietary unionism. This follows because the range of *wealth maximizing* rules or procedures, other things the same, is narrower than the range of rules and procedures consistent with maximizing the utility of rank and file members *across nonproprietary, heterogeneous* unions.[20]

THE RAID

Like publicly held corporations, unions are subject to raiding by other unions. This provides an additional threat to "excessive" managerial discretion. The raid is an attempt by other unions to wrest exclusive bargaining rights from incumbent leaders. The more probable is this threat, other things the same, the higher is the cost to leaders of diverting rents, pecuniary or otherwise, to other interests and away from the rank and file. Presumably raids occur where it is perceived that rank and file members either are or could be persuaded to become dissatisfied with their representation. The raiding union is often the occupant of the same bargain-jurisdiction but affiliated with a different international association; for example, CIO unions have often raided AFL unions. To appropriate revenues from enhanced treasuries, however, requires that raiding managers retain power long enough, in nonproprietary unions, to capture these future benefits. Although this is quite possible, future rewards will be discounted at a higher rate than if capital values could be appropriated in the present. Thus, the threat to managerial discretion from the *raid* should be less intense than in the proprietary, publicly held, corporation or the proprietary union. Moreover, the size of many union organizations is probably smaller than would otherwise be if unions were more proprietary.

Raids also provide opportunities to increase union treasuries with new sources of revenue, to tighten the union grip on employer alternatives (i.e., make the demand for labor more inelastic by eliminating a competitive source of labor) and to spread collective bargaining costs over a larger membership, thus lowering per unit costs to the membership of the raiding union.

To this extent, the raid may provide a relatively quicker way for union managers to expand their discretionary power over resources. Increasing membership by one-third through membership drives may take too long and thus provide benefits too distant relative to an immediate but more costly injection of members through raiding. We will discuss managerial incentives to expand membership in the next section.

Raids may be affected by strikes and picketing against employers until they agree to recognize the raiding union instead of the incumbent. This can be a costly affair for the employer and a drain on the treasuries of both labor organizations. Accordingly, employers and rival unions (i.e., their managements, and members)[21] have great incentive to avoid such dissipation. The National Labor Relations Act lowers the cost of raids for a large fraction of unionized workers. A raiding union covered under the NLRA can call for a representational election if it secures the signatures of 30 percent of the incumbent union's membership. This provision, while protecting union treasuries from rent-dissipating strikes, lowers the costs of raiding to would-be union managers and narrows discretionary boundaries for incumbent leaders. As a consequence, there is some incentive among union leaders to collude. It should not be surprising that *no-raiding* rules and agreements among unions appeared after the passage of the NLRA. In fact, AFL and CIO unions had a no-raiding agreement *before* their merger.[22] Although the agreement was only binding on signatories (104 unions), eventually it was extended to all affiliates of the merged AFL-CIO.[23] It is interesting to note that many of the nonsignatories to this agreement were unions that actually gained members as a result of raiding activities, suggesting a possible trade-off by leaders between growth and the risk of greater control over managerial discretion should it in turn face raids.[24] However, NLRB raiding elections have never represented a very large fraction of all union elections, and this should not be too surprising either.[25] Not only are such elections costly in terms of the resources committed to campaigning, but the raiding nonproprietary union, as we have noted, has no way to capitalize the future stream of benefits arising from the takeover.

MANAGERIAL OBJECTIVES

The question naturally arises, why should the interests of the leadership differ from those of its constituency, the rank and file members of the union? Are not leaders also union members? Are they not most frequently, if not invariably, selected from the working environment of their constituency, and therefore, a reflection of that body? Earlier writers have offered answers in terms of the personal characteristics and role perceptions of those who lead or manage.[26] Of course such characteristics and role perceptions do not really "explain" divergences between the interests of leaders and members, they merely describe different types of behavior on the part of union managers. Although behavioral differences may certainly be affected by the particular preferences or personal motivations of different individuals, such differences are difficult to recognize ex ante. Less difficult is the identification of differences in the cost-reward structures facing individual decision makers. Even if the elements of the utility functions of union leaders and of members were identical,[27] the two groups might still behave differently if they faced different constraints.[28]

Like rank and file members, the union leader has no negotiable right to his union card or to his managerial perquisites. As a result, he is unable to fully capitalize into current transfer prices the present value of future rents that would otherwise come about from current actions he might take. Consequently, those activities will have a smaller payoff relative to actions with more immediate effects. In this sense the constraints facing leaders are little or no different from those facing nonoffice-holding members. However, unless leaders are also employees covered by the collective contract, their salary is usually fixed, at least de jure, by constitutional provision or convention referendum. Although these salaries may in part reflect rents expected by all members and past performances by leaders,[29] they probably do not vary from contract to contract as rents change with strikes and negotiation costs. This suggests that, other things the same, the behavior of union leaders will exhibit significant differences, depending on whether they derive most of their income from employment covered by collective agreement, and function as union officials on a part-time basis,[30] or whether they are paid a full-time straight salary and are not covered or paid under the union's collective agreement. The former group will have objectives and exhibit behavior more in line with rank and file interests than will the latter group.

If leaders fail to share directly in current rents created by wage increments above market levels, they will find it less costly to emphasize other bargaining goals that tend to increase their own welfare. In chapter 5, it was suggested that, absent managerial discretion, the ownership characteristics of nonproprietary unions bias rank and file preferences for rents in favor of current as opposed to deferred payments. That is, the utility maximizing ratio of current payments to deferred payments, for rank and file members (homogeneous preferences), or for the median voter-member (heterogeneous preferences) should be higher in nonproprietary unions than in proprietary unions. Once managerial discretion is introduced this implication is less obvious.

If union managers administer union trust funds, they may and often do determine the interim uses of these funds and/or the financial institutions in which they will be kept. This is, literally, a valuable responsibility, one that can be made to increase the welfare of managers either directly through pecuniary kickbacks from financial intermediaries or through favors, information, introductions to influential people, and other nonpecuniary rent diversions. But even if moral fortitude in managers is so great that such temptations are usually resisted, the salaries of leaders—like the salaries of managers of large corporations—normally are positively correlated with the size of the union's assets, including trust funds, which they administer. Thus managers of nonproprietary unions have the incentive to bias their choices toward contributions to capital accumulation relative to current payments. Although, other things the same, rank and file members may seek to bargain for a "higher" current payment/deferred payment ratio, it is in the interests of leaders to seek a lower one.

Information about the responses of employers to alternative wage demands and to the composition of alternative bargaining packages is costly to discover away from the bargaining table. The leadership, therefore, is provided with an opportunity to change the membership's perception of the parameters that affect them.[31] Consequently, union bargaining goals are more likely to approach configurations consistent with, or closer to, leadership preferences. Even if members have the opportunity to compare their settlement with those obtained by other unions, managers likewise have the opportunity to influence those comparisons. The selection of suitable comparisons is not the only way a leader convinces his membership that he has done a good job, but it is an important aspect of collective bargaining.[32]

Figure 6.1 describes the relationship between a union leader's preferences and those of the rank and file, as expressed by the median voter, for current vs. deferred payment components in the bargaining package. Panel A contains a maximum rent curve in terms of the ratio of deferred payments to current payments. Total rents, ϱ_T, are shown on the ordinate axis and the ratio of deferred payments (d.p.) to current payments (c.p.) is shown on the abscissa. Superimposed on the A panel is the leader's preference function. The preference direction is northeast, so that more rents and more deferred payments relative to current payments enhance his utility.

If we assume that the union has a nonproprietary structure, and if the costs of detecting and policing deviations from rank and file objectives are positive, the relevant constraint facing the leader is the negatively sloped portion of the total rent curve in panel A. Utility is maximized for the union leader, at payment ratio a″. Note that a″ constitutes a higher ratio of deferred to current payments than at ā, where rents are maximized. Moreover, a″ is not consistent with utility maximization for the rank and file, as reflected in the utility function of the median voter in panel C. The point a″ in panel A may be projected on to panel C by means of the rent distribution function $m(\varrho_m)$, with slope $1/m$, located in panel D. The larger is m the more steeply sloped the distribution function and the smaller the amount of rent available to any given union member. The equivalent of a″ in median-voter utility space, given the distribution function, is at c″. Constrained by his rent function, the median voter at c″ may only reach utility level U″U″.

Compare this result to one where there are zero costs of detecting deviations by union leaders from rank and file objectives. Information acquisition and enforcement are costless activities to

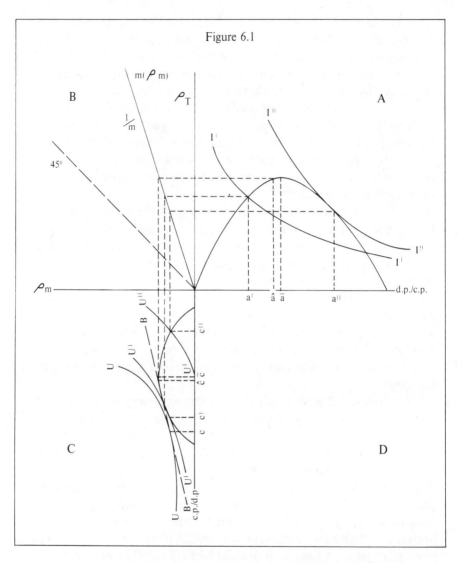

Figure 6.1

members. As a consequence, payment ratios that conflict with utility maximization for the median voter will be rejected in the bargaining package negotiated by leaders and therefore constitute a threat to their incumbency. In panel C, utility is maximized at c′, at utility level U′U′. With costless monitoring, the slope of the constraint facing the union leader in panel A will be infinite at payment ratios beyond a′, limiting him to utility level I′I′.[33]

For reasons developed in the last two chapters, members of a proprietary union are better situated to capture the improvement in welfare that would arise from policing the discretion of union leaders. This implies that members of such a union will be willing to devote relatively more resources to the monitoring function than their nonproprietary counterparts. This in turn suggests that leaders, in the proprietary unions, will make collective bargaining choices more in conformity with the utility maximization interests of their membership. Thus, we should expect that current/deferred payment ratios will differ between the proprietary and nonproprietary union. Moreover, we can expect that the payment ratio in the proprietary union will be closer to the ratio that maximizes rents than the ratio to be found in the nonproprietary union. This can be seen from an examination of panels A and C in figure 6.1. In panel C, the line BB represents the market rate for the sale or lease of membership rights in a proprietary union. If the preferences of a majority of members, in this union, differ from the payment ratio that maximizes rents, they can always sell or lease their property to others having preferences more consistent with maximum rent. At a price such as BB, the median-voter member agrees to choose payment ratio c, desired by a minority of members. The ratio c, however, is not the *effective* ratio of current to deferred payments consumed by the median voter. The payment to him in exchange for his vote allows him to reach a higher level of utility UU than he could otherwise achieve without proprietary rights in membership status. Under these assumptions, utility is maximized for the median voter at c. Thus the payment ratio for which leaders in a proprietary union will be authorized to bargain will be closer to the ratio that maximizes rent than will be the case in a nonproprietary union. This is demonstrated by projecting the payment ratio in panel C at $\hat{c}$ on to panel A at $\hat{a}$. Since members of proprietary unions may capture the gains from monitoring leadership discretion, the slope of the opportunity set in panel A is infinite for all payment ratios beyond $\hat{a}$. From panel A, it can be seen that nonproprietary unions imply a relatively higher ratio of deferred to current payments (a″) and smaller rents than are implied by the proprietary form of unionization ($\hat{a}$).

Taking the analysis one step further, it may be argued that since proprietary rights in membership and voting permit the effective choice of *any* payment ratio, the median voter will be unwilling to sacrifice any rent for alternative ratios of current to deferred payments. In other words, his indifference curves will appear horizontal in panel C and utility will be maximized at c̄. Leaders will face an infinite constraint, in panel A, at ā, where monopoly rent for the organization is maximized.

The above analysis also yields implications for comparisons between payment ratios in ununionized firms and unionized firms organized by nonproprietary unions. Assume that nonunion workers and nonproprietary union members have tastes for current and deferred payments that, although different in terms of absolute levels, are approximately the same in relative terms. Then, if the costs of monitoring union managers are positive, we should expect to observe a higher ratio of deferred payments to current payments among nonproprietary union workers relative to nonunion workers.[34] This follows from our analysis in figure 6.1 and from our analysis in chapter five. Employers in ununionized firms will purchase labor at competitive payment ratios, with the view of attracting the marginal worker, while employers in unionized firms will face the collective bargaining demands of union leaders seeking to shift current payments to deferred payments.[35]

UNION MANAGERS AND WAGE-MEMBERSHIP POLICY

The discussion above has focused on current payments (usually in the form of money wage rates) *relative* to deferred payments. Analyses of managerial discretion in nonproprietary unions, however, are also relevant in explaining the *level* of remuneration per worker, whether it relates to money-wage payments or to the dollar value of supplements. Under the assumptions used in chapter five,[36] it was argued that incumbent members of nonproprietary unions would respond to an increase in the demand for labor by seeking wage levels that would encourage employers to limit employment at or near the existing membership. This appears to be contrary to observed behavior in most labor unions.[37] Increases in demand appear to be positively correlated with the expansion of both employment and of union membership in unionized industries. Either it is the case that members of these unions own a great deal more proprietary rights than suspected (and therefore the returns to monitoring managerial discretion are "high"), or some other factors are operating. This section seeks to identify some of the latter.

There are several factors that encourage union managers, in the face of increased demand for labor, to bargain for wage rates and other worker remuneration so that employment and membership may expand beyond existing levels. These factors include the effects of expanded employment and membership on leader salaries, union treasuries, tenure, and the leader's relationship with the employer. The salaries of union leaders are, in part, positively associated with the membership size of the unions they administer and the value of union assets.[38] Since the initiation fees and dues in most unions are either fixed by constitution, or subject to change only at the will of the majority of members, managers have an incentive to expand membership when possible. "Large" memberships often mean "large" treasuries, from which to finance expense accounts and purchase assets. The larger memberships sought by leaders are at the expense of higher wage rates for incumbents. The sacrifice of potential rents in terms of foregone wage differentials does not directly constrain union managers, because they rarely share in them.[39] If salaries of managers did vary directly, with current rents obtained by members through wage differentials, managers would still find it attractive—at the margin—to trade *some* of this reward for both (somewhat) higher executive salaries associated with larger memberships *and* the nontaxable benefits that come with control over larger treasuries and trust funds.

Union managers may also be expected to pursue wage policies that expand membership in response to increased labor demand if larger memberships raise the cost of forming voting blocs strong enough to threaten the managers' political survival. The larger the membership, the smaller the returns to any one member of devoting resources to collective action. Moreover, the larger the membership, the more likely it is to have *heterogeneous* interests. Although this may make it more difficult for managers to identify the median voter, on any issue, it will also make it more costly to form coalitions of voting blocs.[40] To my knowledge this is the first time such an argument has been used to explain at least some of the leadership's interest in the growth of the organization.[41]

Of course, the foregoing arguments assume that the membership does not vote on each and every element in the collective bargaining package as a separate item. Otherwise, it would be extremely difficult for managerial preferences to overshadow the revealed sentiment of the membership. This kind of voting, however, is prohibitively costly. If ratification by members or by delegates is required before collective agreements may be executed, it is the entire package that is accepted or rejected. This makes less popular features of contracts more costly to oppose, giving leaders a freer hand. If membership ratification of collective bargaining agreements is not required,[42] leaders must at least be careful to adopt policies that yield utility to a significant proportion of members above some *critical* level.[43]

However, if minority subgroups in the membership are allowed to form their own election units within the union, and to flirt with rival unions,[44] the incumbent leadership may be forced to consider the utilities of median voters of several different groups. For example, assume that the critical utility level of the median voter in a minority subgroup is associated with collective bargaining demands that are more costly to the employer than demands made by the median voter in the majority group. To retain the allegiance of the former group, who might otherwise associate with a rival union, union bargaining objectives may have to reflect higher wage rates and other payments that result in longer strikes and fewer employment opportunities facing *all* of the membership. If subgroup demands threaten the allegiance of the majority group, however, leaders will be induced to let the minority group find another union.[45] The prospect of generating Globetype election units as membership expands should act to place limits on managerial interests in membership as a source of utility.

The relatively more moderate stance of the leader, in the face of growing labor demand, may yield for him the benefits of employer gratitude, in addition to large employment and memberships. Collective agreements that tend to suppress wage rates and other payment per worker at the expense of at least some incumbent members have been termed, pejoratively, *sweetheart contracts*. The more notorious arrangements were exposed during the McClellan hearings of the 1950s,[46] revealing instances of employers making pecuniary payments directly to union leaders in exchange for assurances against strikes and "excessive" wage demands. Yet, the incentives for such behavior differ only in degree from the incentives of union leaders to "get along" with their counterparts across the bargaining table and to "maintain good relations"[47] with them.

"Good relations" are a source of utility to union managers because they indirectly yield both pecuniary and nonpecuniary rewards. Employers may be more willing to make "loans" to union managers, to introduce them to persons more willing to be their creditors, to introduce them to prestigious individuals with whom they will be able to socialize outside their work environment, or who will provide valuable information at favorable terms. Likewise, "moderate" and "responsible" behavior also appeals to politicians. It relieves political pressures to "do something" about "irresponsible" wage demands.[48] The more costly it is for members to know just what is attainable, and the more costly it is for them to police or monitor managerial discretion, the greater the opportunity for leaders to trade off one source of utility—the rewards associated with higher rents for members, for another source—the rewards associated with maintaining "good relations" with management and government.

The leadership has symmetrical interests in membership size in the face of a decline in demand, but it should meet with relatively greater resistance from rank and file members. Universal wage cuts, in response to *negative* demand changes, to maintain employment and therefore membership at or near existing levels will be more clearly perceived as threatening to the interests of the more senior members of the union than will "moderate" as opposed to "higher" wage increases in response to *positive* demand changes. Without costless information about what is attainable, it is not clear to rank and file workers what constitutes a "moderate" wage demand. So long as leaders are able to achieve increases in real income for their members, they are in a position—though not always a strong one—to argue that this is the best of all possible worlds. But a wage cut to members not immediately threatened by unemployment is a clear signal that their real incomes are now lower than they have to be.

Wage concessions will be resisted, by the median voter, until the expected utility from resisting a wage cut is less than the utility of income earned after such a cut. Even if new contracts do not require membership ratification, in the long run, wage policy at the bargaining table must be consistent with the political survival of the union's leaders (i.e., consistent with some critical level of utility associated with median preferences). This is in accord with the popular observation that union wage policy is rather asymmetrical, in that wage cuts frequently are resisted even though some members will lose their jobs. On the other hand, the existence of some managerial discretion, in negotiating wage contracts, allows leaders to pursue the retention of existing membership levels against the will of the majority of members without immediate political setbacks. We should expect union wage policy to be relatively rigid downward *but not completely so.* That is, we should expect wage reductions in nonproprietary unions to *lag* downward relative to policies in proprietary unions and in the nonunionized markets.

Once again, in unions where managers are monitored more closely, where rival unions (and/or internal opposition) are more "competitive," downward wage flexibility should be less obvious, ceteris paribus. This may explain why some scholars could claim that some unions appear to be either oblivious to the employment consequences of their wage policies, while simultaneously other scholars found unions to be very perceptive of and responsive to those consequences.[49]

SUMMARY

Although members and leaders have the same nonproprietary rights in membership status, differences in other costs and rewards facing these groups, respectively, suggest a divergence of interests that can only be policed at some positive cost to the rank and file. The higher this cost the more discretion (up to some critical level) leaders may exercise in formulating and executing union policy. This potential intraunion conflict together with the nonproprietary nature of most union organizations yields implications that are capable of refutation. They are:

(a) The tenure of officials in nonproprietary unions should be longer and the frequency of contested elections should be lower than experienced in proprietary organizations that elect their officers by shareholder or member vote.

(b) Relatively more managerial activities and functions in nonproprietary unions will be monitored by formal rules and regulations than will managerial activities in proprietary organizations.

(c) Nonproprietary unions will exhibit a relatively wider variety of formal rules governing their internal management than will proprietary organizations of similar size, measured by shareholders or members.

(d) The asset structure and investment policies of most nonproprietary unions will appear very conservative when compared with proprietary organizations of similar ownership size (shareholders or members).

(e) Managers in nonproprietary unions with relatively high monitoring costs will be expected to ration the market allocation of union assets at nonmarket clearing rates, thus transfering wealth away from members toward themselves.

(f) Nonproprietary unions will adopt a relatively higher ratio of deferred to current payments in establishing bargaining policies when compared with unions possessing relatively more proprietary characteristics.

(g) Nonproprietary unions will adopt a relatively higher ratio of deferred to current payments in their bargaining policies when compared to the deferred/current payment ratios of workers in ununionized firms.

(h) In those nonproprietary unions where policing and monitoring costs of the union's leadership are relatively high, employment rigidities under conditions of rising labor demand, and wage rigidities under conditions of declining labor demand, will be relatively less pronounced than in other nonproprietary unions.

(i) Nonproprietary unions with relatively high costs of monitoring leaders will exhibit relatively more wildcat strikes and other unauthorized collective action.

(j) The threat of merger and raiding activities among nonproprietary unions should be a relatively less important constraint on union managerial discretion than such activities would be in proprietary organizations.

7

Price and Nonprice Rationing of Union Memberships

THE PROPRIETARY CASE

Much of the analysis of chapter four, dealing with wage-membership policy under proprietary unionism, turns on the ability and incentives of incumbent members to participate in the rents that would otherwise go to new members. Perhaps the most obvious participatory policy would be to charge subsequent members a lump sum fee, reflecting the present value of the expected rents produced by union efforts, and then share that fee among incumbents according to some formula. The fee (F) may be expressed as $F = \frac{by}{r}[1 - (1 + r)^{-n}]$.[1] Assume that incumbent members share F equally. Then each incumbent could receive $S = \frac{tF}{r}[1 - (1 + r)^{-n}]$, where t is the ratio of new members to old and n is the number of years a member expects rents to continue. The value of each incumbent member's job right is increased by S times the number of additional members. Since, in proprietary terms, job rights are salable, it is in the interests of incumbents to expand membership whenever increments in rents are possible. This analysis also suggests that where wage discrimination is economical, either among a number of employers (i.e., second degree discrimination) or with respect to one employer (i.e., first degree discrimination),[2] the prospect of appropriating more rents will encourage even larger additions to membership than under uniform wage policies.

For new members, the purchase of a union card at a single lump sum price is equivalent to the purchase of any specialized asset that yields some receipt stream over time. Since a proprietary membership card is transferable, the would-be member's access to the capital markets for funds to purchase the card should be no more difficult (costly) than his access to the same markets if he were, instead, financing a taxi medallion or the purchase of a radio station with its attendant license.[3] In fact, this was the predominant way ownership shares were sold in worker-owned plywood co-ops.[4]

Three independent considerations may operate to alter the above single-lump payment scheme. First, to the extent that the union can negotiate lower interest rates than can its members acting individually,[5] the total price it will demand for membership will be lower than otherwise by an amount something less than the total interest savings. Rather than a simple entry fee, new members will make periodic payments to the union, acting as financial intermediary, that will include the remainder of the interest savings. Second, as with other income yielding assets, the stream of rents associated with union membership is not a certain one. Given a degree of risk aversion, the fee potential members would be willing to pay after accounting for uncertainty[6] may be smaller than the rents that could be extracted from new members if some of those risks were shifted, spread and pooled among the existing membership.[7] One way to accommodate risk aversion is to set the initiation fee relatively low and extract the rest of the rents through some income contingent charge. This charge will be higher than the opportunity cost of the income that would have otherwise been at the disposal of the union had a one-time inititation fee been levied.[8] Roughly 20 percent of the worker-owned plywood co-ops studied by Berman (1967)[9] financed ownership shares this way. This suggests that periodic charges levied against members would differ by tenure in membership and by income, although union services to all members might be identical. Alternatively, periodic charges could be kept uniform to all members but services supplied to new members would be fewer or less valuable. More generally, so long as differences in periodic charges are *not* proportional to differences in the value of services supplied as between new members and incumbents, the latter may extract monopoly rents from the former, as the price of entry, without the exclusive use of lump sum initiation fees.[10]

Finally, wage and hours differentials and fringe benefit differentials between incumbents and newer members, based on criteria other than differences in productivity, provide a source of rent transfers that may also economize on the finance costs and risks to new members of buying entry in one lump sum fee. For example, if "skill" differentials are determined by seniority alone, rents are being appropriated from newer members to incumbents.[11] But rent transferring wage differentials pose problems for the union in that firms may seek to substitute toward the lower paid worker.[12] This fear has long been recognized by unions and constitutes an important reason for their attention to wage rate standardization within a given occupation or job classification covered by collective contract. We may, therefore, expect proprietary unions to adopt hours and dues differentials, as a means of transferring rent between incumbents and newcomers, but we do not expect to observe *discriminatory* wage differentials. Nevertheless, the proprietary model does not imply that the narrowing of *productivity justified* skill differentials, in the interests of wage standardization, is consistent with the maximization of union monopoly rent. Yet, recent evidence suggests that unions, paradoxically, appear to *narrow* wage differentials between skilled and less skilled members.[13]

The choice between lump sum fees, two-part tariffs, and wage differentials is not governed merely by the economies of risk spreading or capital market disparities, although, other things the same, the absence of risk and of transaction costs would leave no objective criterion for choosing between these methods of pricing memberships.[14] Income-contingent and fixed periodic fees, whether direct or indirect, will affect choice between work and nonwork at the margin, and affect the fraction of potential rents which incumbents can extract. It will be in the union's interest (i.e., incumbents) to devote resources to monitoring and policing the work efforts of new members up to expected losses in rents. However, the more extensive is the monitoring the more costly is this arrangement.[15] If the economies of risk pooling and spreading, net of monitoring costs and adjusted for forsaken interest earnings, yield rents larger than those represented by one-time entry fees (lowered by the premium necessary to attract risk averse buyers), two-part tariffs and/or remuneration differentials will be chosen over single fees. Whatever the choice of pricing regime, the proprietary model implies that the present value of membership pricing will reflect the present value of the rent stream associated with union membership and be reflected in the market value of a union card.

PRICE DISCRIMINATION IN MEMBERSHIPS

The analysis so far has ignored the possibility of differential rents among union applicants. Rent differentials may arise either because the union is a price discriminator among different employers in the labor market, or because would-be members have different opportunity costs, or both. In any event, a proprietary union seeking to maximize rents would find it in its interests to discriminate in pricing memberships.[16] Abstracting from risk aversion, and assuming zero transaction costs, the ideal discriminatory scheme would appear to be the sale of job rights at different lump sum prices reflecting differences in expected rents. However, unless unions can prevent new members with relatively high opportunity costs from reselling their cards to would-be members with relatively lower opportunity costs, ceteris paribus, price discrimination of this sort is doomed to failure. Rather than price all union cards at the lowest rent expected, so as not to exclude a possible buyer (or risk resale among members) the union, constrained by the threat of arbitrage, could extract even greater total rents by charging a uniform two-part tariff. Alternatively, discrimination can be affected through wage differentials applied to new members.[17] Thus, analogous to the more discriminatory pricing regimes discussed above, the existence of both uncertainty and *rent differentials,* together with positive costs of contracting, constitute the necessary conditions for the existence of nonlump sum differential pricing of memberships in proprietary unions.

THE NONPROPRIETARY CASE

The evidence does not support the proprietary implication that the present value of initiation fees, dues and other assessments should reflect the monopoly value of rents generated by union activity. Taft (1956), Becker (1959), and Pencavel (1971) have found that both initiation fees *and* dues are, with exceptions, much lower than would be justified by the estimated monopoly value of membership status. In a 1963 survey of initiation fees reported to the Bureau of Labor Statistics by 2,739 local unions, only 8.8 percent required a fee in excess of $50.[18] This is rather remarkable when it is known that the union/nonunion average wage differential has been estimated at between 10 percent and 15 percent.[19] The present value of a monopoly wage differential of 10 percent applied to the average union worker's income should be several times greater than $50.[20] Similarly, only 1 percent of these local unions reported dues in excess of $10 per month.[21] Moreover, dues are rarely levied on an income contingent basis, as implied by the proprietary model discussed above, where applicants were assumed to be risk averse.

Returning to initiation fees, Becker, for example, noted that taxicab medallions in New York City sold for prices that reflected the capitalized value of monopoly rents, made possible by legal restrictions on market entry.[22] In contrast, the glazers union, with one of the highest initiation fees among American trade unions ($3,000), charge only a small fraction of the estimated monopoly value of membership status.[23]

A few explanations for this pervasive anomaly have been offered in the literature. One is that there are laws against "excessive" fees charged by labor unions.[24] But "low" fees existed before the Taft-Hartley strictures. Another is that the power of trade unions is generally supported by government, largely associated with the New Deal labor legislation of the 1930s. Such aid may be withdrawn or modified, as in the case of post-World War II labor legislation, after union abuses became widely known. To the extent that the monopoly power of unions may be flaunted in the "face of the public" by initiation fees that reflect the high personal gain members can expect from their organizations, public opinion may sour and the government's support will be partially withdrawn. Thus, it is said, fees are kept "low".[25] The explanation ignores the fact that other groups rely on government aid, in the sense discussed, but are content to ignore the possibility of public outrage. Taxi drivers, liquor retailers, broadcasters, and airline owners, are but a few examples.

A more appealing explanation of the "underpricing" of memberships, focuses on ownership differences between union members and other monopolists. Would-be taxi medallion owners, broadcast and liquor store licensees all seek to own a transferable asset. Would-be unionists, on the other hand, seek to acquire a nontransferable asset. I conjecture the nontransferable characteristic of union membership more nearly explains entry pricing among unions than do the explanations offered above. Two factors tend to

suppress the price of entry below the present value of the anticipated rent stream. First, without further evidence of financial
worth, lending institutions would be less than eager to finance the
purchase of a nontransferable union card. Other things the same,
the effective demand for membership and the price of entry should
be lower, absent such financing, than would be warranted by the
actual monopoly value of being a union member. Second, even if
capital market financing were available, at no premium, union
applicants would be less than willing to prepay the full monopoly
value of nontransferable memberships unless they expected to live
and work long enough to earn a normal return on their
investments.

It should be immediately objected, however, that the union itself would finance membership acquisition by applicants and levy
some periodic charge against the monopoly wage of entrants. The
present value of the periodic payment would be set equal to the
capital value of membership status plus the union's incremental
cost of handling such a loan.[26] But this objection ignores a third
and most important factor. The nonproprietary status of union
membership precludes personal claims to revenues generated from
the sale of new memberships, and therefore prevents incumbents
from capitalizing such revenue streams into enhanced market
values for their own membership rights. Accordingly, incumbents
have limited incentives to support policies that structure fees, dues
and other assessments, even wage and benefit differentials, so that
the *present value* of rents are maximized. That is, once multiperiod
alternatives and decisions become relevant, so that current actions
have *future* consequences, ownership characteristics will influence
the level and mix of fees, dues, and indirect prices of union
membership.

For example, since incumbents cannot appropriate revenues
from the sale of memberships at market clearing prices, some non-
revenue generated sources of utility are relatively less costly to pursue. The pursuit of one such source suggests that existing members
may keep initiation fees below market-clearing levels, so that they
can promote excess demands for entry and thereby select new
members on the basis of criteria that promises to enhance the utility of incumbents. Obvious examples include the racial, religious,
national, and sexual characteristics of would-be members. The
incidence of nonprice rationing among unions is discussed below.

In a nonproprietary union, rents not claimed in the present are not secure if left to the future. Although incumbents cannot appropriate current revenues from the sale of new memberships, they do have an incentive to seek policies that divert current rents *directly* and *immediately* away from newer members, and direct the union's treasury toward themselves. For example, direct and immediate forms of pecuniary transfers include: wage and hours differentials between senior and junior members that are greater than their respective productivity differentials; regressive dues schedules among members of different tenure, as in the case where dues are inversely proportional to the wages of members ranked by length of ownership; senior-junior differentials in the probability of layoff; and discriminatory benefit programs that favor senior members though disproportionately financed by junior members.

It is important to note that the above senior-junior differentials, implied by the nonproprietary model, differ significantly from the differentials discussed under proprietary unionism. In the latter case, wage rate and other differentials represent periodic transfers that are based on the *present value* of monopoly rents that employee-members can anticipate. Differentials calculated under nonproprietary unionism, on the other hand, are based on the level of rents new members can anticipate in the current period only. Thus the two models do not predict the same results. Given the same capital value of union monopoly rents, nonproprietary unions should exhibit larger current period differentials between incumbents and newer members than proprietary unions. However, incumbent members of the latter will enjoy greater wealth because of their ability to capture the capitalized value of differentials in the market value of their union status.

Although wage differentials are an obvious means of current rent transfers between senior and junior members, they have, as in the analysis of proprietary unions discussed above, the unfortunate effect of influencing employer input decisions at the margin. Thus, wage differentials beyond those warranted by productivity differentials, run the risk of threatening the cohesion of the union as a cartel. Differentials that favor incumbents may encourage employers to substitute away from the former toward junior worker-members. Efforts to prevent such substitutions will require resources and therefore place pressure on members in the form of higher dues payments.[27] These problems do not arise if differentials favoring incumbents are established in dues payments, union financed benefits, and the probability of layoffs. Significantly, Rosen, Freeman (1977), and Heckman and Neumann, have written that union wage policy, far from transferring rents away from new members toward incumbents, appears to support redistribution toward less skilled and younger members.[28]

In a recent study, Medoff (1979) found that layoffs were used relatively more intensively in unionized firms and that between 58 and 78 percent of the relevant workers covered by the collective bargaining agreements he studied indicated that "seniority was the 'sole' or 'primary' factor in determining layoff rights."[29] Medoff explains this phenomenon in terms of differences in the attitudes of senior and junior members toward layoffs, and the dominance of the former group in the voting regimes of labor unions. Our theory identifies this predominant layoff convention as an auxiliary device allowing incumbents to transfer union rents *directly* and *immediately* from junior members.[30] It is a device used instead of significant wage differentials. Layoff differentials, dues differentials and benefit differentials may thus help explain the persistence of the wage equalizing phenomena among unions that scholars have long reported[31] but only recently documented.[32] Although unions appear to adopt wage rate equalizing policies within occupations and across organized firms,[33] offsetting nonwage differentials between incumbents and newer members may, in the final analysis, transfer *current* rents toward the former and away from the latter as economic theory would suggest.

COMPETITION FOR RENTS BY UNION LEADERS

Like their rank and file constituency, union managers have no *proprietary* claim to revenues generated from the pricing of memberships. However, their strategic position as financial wardens gives them more than a passing interest in the formation of membership pricing policy. As discussed in chapter six, a manager's policy toward membership *size* is affected by his inability to independently determine initiation fees and dues. Price setting is usually done by convention referendum or by delegate vote. As a result, managers have the incentive to increase general revenues by moderating demand induced wage increases and expanding memberships beyond existing levels at rank and file determined fees. But this argument is too rigid. Leaders do not accept the price of membership as given. They would clearly be better off with larger memberships[34] *and* larger treasuries. To the extent that the incomes of members contain significant rents, the elasticity of demand for membership should be relatively low and the potentially transferrable rents relatively large.[35] This perhaps explains the perennial tension between members and their leaders over the question of raising dues rates. The former are invariably against such raises and the latter are ever devising ways to achieve them. For example, most dues receipts are used not to maintain the organization, or to pay strike benefits or the salaries of officers and staff, but rather to pay premiums on life insurance, medical and hospital insurance, pensions, supplemental unemployment payments[36] and other *private* benefits that will attract the dollars of the rank and file.[37]

It is not a coincidence that the benefits sold to members via higher dues are those for which the union has some monopoly advantage. Much of the insurance it provides members is particularly suited to the economies of group rates. Unions are composed of large groups of individuals who work in similar environments, often belong to the same race and sex, and possess similar educational backgrounds. Although the organization of information about such groups for the purposes of selling insurance may otherwise be relatively costly, unions collect this information for other purposes and thus may reproduce it at almost zero cost.[38] Thus, the sale of insurance programs to members in exchange for higher fees and dues also produces positive net revenues for union treasuries. Not all leaders are successful in using initiation fees and dues rates to increase treasuries. The probability of success will be greater in the more nonproprietary unions, and in those unions with high costs of monitoring managerial discretion.

NONPRICE RATIONING IN A NONPROPRIETARY UNION

One of the implications that may be derived from the analysis of proprietary unionism developed in chapter 4 is that, other things the same, nonprice rationing is less likely to occur in unions with relatively large potential rents and relatively small numbers of incumbent members.[39] The evidence, however, does not seem to support this implication. It is widely believed that craft unions with relatively small memberships and relatively large rents per member practice relatively more nonprice rationing in the form of racial and sexual discrimination among applicants to their ranks than do industrial unions with, usually, larger memberships.[40] It has been suggested by Ashenfelter (1973) that this observation can be explained by the fact that, unlike craft unions, industrial unions are often found in relatively unskilled labor markets where there is a higher incidence of nonwhite and female workers. Exclusion of the latter two groups from membership would impose a competitive threat to the survival of such unions. Ashenfelter has concluded that, in such circumstances, heavily unionized markets would exhibit egalitarian membership policies; otherwise these markets would be only lightly unionized, if at all (the South being an example in point). Merely to observe, however, that nonwhites are more represented in industrial than in craft unions ignores the fact that the former have been known to employ separate locals for blacks, separate seniority lists, and separate promotion lists; and that these separations serve to relegate nonwhites to lower earnings opportunities.[41]

Given the assumptions of the nonproprietary model, it should be no surprise that nonprice rationing in membership and access to job opportunities would be found in both craft *and* industrial unions. In a nonproprietary union, institutional arrangements make it prohibitively costly to appropriate rents other than those capturable through current wage, hours and benefit differentials. The effective price of buying "desirable" personal characteristics in new members is relatively lower than if all potential rents were readily (inexpensively) capturable. Recall expression (7'), presented in chapter five, and allow the following modification:

$$\frac{\theta \partial u / \partial g_i}{\theta \partial u / \partial g_j} = \frac{-\alpha \partial \varrho_m / \partial g_i}{P_j - \alpha \partial \varrho_m / \partial g_j} \tag{8'}$$

Assume that g_i is a personal characteristic that is desired in new members and that is available to all incumbent members at a zero market price. Let g_j be some other element in the G_1 vector, with private good characteristics. Assume also that, at the margin, $\partial \varrho_m / \partial g_i < 0$ and $\partial \varrho_m / \partial g_j > 0$. In the perfect proprietary case, where $\alpha = 1$, the *effective* price of g_i is positive and measures the full costs of choosing this personal quality relative to choosing more of g_j (and thus more rents), the private good in the bargaining package. Once the proprietary assumption is relaxed, so that $\alpha < 1$, both numerator and denominator in (8') fall; but the numerator falls more than proportionately relative to the denominator. The result is to lower the relative *effective* price of desirable personal characteristics, a collective good to members, and thus more is consumed at the expense of rent-increasing op-portunities.[42] The fact that current rents may be directly cap-turable through wage, hours, layoff and benefit differentials does not in any way alter the above implication. Since membership sta-tus is not transferable, differentials cannot be capitalized into the present and thus distant returns will be heavily discounted. The ef-fect is to weaken the connection between nonprice rationing and loss of monopoly rents.

The objection may be raised that this analysis does not apply to industrial unions because the latter are rarely in a position to ex-clude "undesirable" would-be members. Employers have already hired them under union shop agreements. Other things the same, however, economic theory would predict no significant difference in the degree of discrimination exhibited in the membership poli-cies of nonproprietary craft and industrial unions. In fact, the evi-dence presented by Ashenfelter and others, purporting to identify differential discrimination within craft and industrial unions, is less than persuasive. This is so because it fails to focus on an impli-cation that arises from a fundamental distinction between referral unions, typically craft unions, and nonreferral unions, typically industrial unions.[43] Membership policy under referral unionism is influenced by the power to control the supply of workers to a particular trade or group of trades rather than to a specific firm. Nonprice rationing in the hiring and allocation of workers, as a consequence, would reveal itself in the *exclusion* of undesirable would-be unionists. On the other hand, nonreferral unions, be-cause their unit of organization is the firm or industry, rather than the trade or occupation, seek *inclusivity* in their membership poli-cies. That is, given the level of employment in the firm or industry, industrial unions are motivated—subject to cost constraints—to include all employees as members. In this environment, nonprice discrimination will reveal itself not in terms of the exclusion of non-whites from the union, but rather in terms of the exclusion of non-whites from seniority lists and promotion lists favored by whites, and the assignment of nonwhites to seniority and promotion lists promising relatively inferior economic opportunities.

Therefore, even if industrial unions were not subject to the threat of relatively large concentrations of nonwhite workers, which forces them toward more egalitarianism, craft unions would appear more discriminatory by exhibiting a smaller proportion of non-whites in their membership relative to industrial unions. Since discrimination by *exclusion* is employed mostly by craft unions, whereas discrimination in industrial unions takes another less obvious form, the nonreferral union is left with the *appearance* of a more egalitarian posture.[44] This posture is accentuated in those markets where the fraction of nonwhites in industrial union jurisdictions, both prior and subsequent to unionization, is much larger than in the case of craft union jurisdictions.

SUMMARY

For some time the underpricing of union memberships and the modest dues requirements of most labor organizations have been puzzling phenomena for both institutional and theoretical labor economists. Tempting explanations focusing on legal prohibitions and egalitarian sentiments of rank and file members have never quite achieved general acceptance. This chapter has offered an alternative hypothesis that focuses on the ownership characteristics of labor unions that operate to encourage the rationing of memberships at less than market clearing prices. The model of the nonproprietary union, as developed from earlier chapters, predicts that: (a) initiation fees will be set below market clearing levels; (b) dues, benefits, hours, and layoff differentials will favor incumbent workers; (c) the present value of the sum of all new member payments into a nonproprietary union's treasury will be lower than the capitalized value of the stream of monopoly rents anticipated by new members as a group; (d) nonprice rationing schemes will employ criteria relevant to the utility of currently employed rank and file members, such as race, nationality, religion, politics, sex, etc.; (e) ownership characteristics and not union classification (craft vs. industrial) are relevant in determining rationing criteria in allocating union monopoly rents among would-be recipients.

Notes

1. INTRODUCTION

1. John Dunlop, *Wage Determination Under Trade Unionism* (New York: Mac-Millan Co., 1944).
2. Ibid.; Henry Simons, "Some Reflections on Syndicalism," in *Economic Policy for a Free Society* (Chicago: University of Chicago Press, 1948).
3. William Fellner, *Competition Among the Few* (New York: A.A. Knopf, 1949); Alan Cartter, *Theory of Wages and Employment* (Homewood: R.D. Irwin, 1959); Wallace Atherton, *Theory of Union Bargaining Goals* (Princeton, N.J.: Princeton University Press, 1973).
4. Dunlop, *Wage Determination;* John Powel, *A Theory of Union Behavior Applied to the Medical Profession,* Ph.D. diss., University of Washington, 1973 (unpublished).
5. John Dunlop, *Wage Determination.*
6. Arthur Ross, *Trade Union Wage Policy* (Berkeley and Los Angeles: University of California Press, 1956); Wallace Atherton, *Union Bargaining Goals.*
7. Arthur Ross, *Wage Policy.*
8. Monroe Berkowitz, "The Economics of Trade Union Organization and Administration," *Industrial and Labor Relations Review* 7 (July 1954): 575-92; Wallace Atherton, Union Bargaining Goals.
9. Melvin Reder, "Job Scarcity and the Nature of Union Power," *Industrial and Labor Relations Review* 13 (April 1960): 349-62.
10. But see Gary S. Becker, "Union Restrictions on Entry," in *The Public Stake in Union Power*, ed. Philip D. Bradley (Charlottesville: University Press of Virginia, 1959) for an alternative measure of union monopoly power.
11. See H. Gregg Lewis, "Competition and Monopoly Unionism," in *The Public Stake in Union Power,* ed. Philip D. Bradley (Charlottesville: University Press of Virginia, 1959) and Powel, *Theory of Union Behavior,* for wealth-maximizing models of union behavior.
12. See Harold Demsetz, "Some Aspects of Property Rights," *Journal of Law and Economics* 9 (October 1966): 61-70.
13. A comprehensive survey of empirical studies bearing on the economic theory of property rights has been written by Louis De Alessi. See "The Economics of Property Rights: A Review of the Evidence," *Research in Law and Economics* 2 (Spring 1980).
14. Ibid.
15. Their models, together with several others, are also critiqued in chap. 2.
16. George E. Johnson, "Economic Analysis of Trade Unionism," *American Economic Review* 65 (May 1975): 23-28.

2. A CRITIQUE OF THE THEORETICAL LITERATURE

1. Note that the services provided by unions to their members are not too dissimilar from the services provided by theatrical or booking agents to entertainers. The actors hire agents to negotiate contracts that specify many elements, including price and working conditions. The agents do not pay the actors from earnings derived from the sale of actor services to studio-employers. Yet, few would argue that agents are thereby unable to maximize the wealth of their clients because they do not sell anything to employers. Recently, actors have formed their own agencies. Perhaps, for this subgroup the analogy is even stronger. To my knowledge, this analogy was first pointed out by Gene L. Chapin in "The Union as an Economic Enterprise: An Exploratory Essay," Ohio University Department of Economics, 1971 (unpublished).

2. See Dunlop, *Wage Determination*, pp. 33 and 41; Ross, *Wage Policy*, p. 28; Fellner, *Competition*, p. 255; Edward Mason, "Labor Monopoly and All That," *Industrial Relations Research Association Proceedings*, December 1955, pp. 192–194; Cartter, *Theory of Wages*, pp. 80–82.

3. The wage bill is defined as the product of the wage rate (per annum) and the total number of members employed.

4. It should be noted that Dunlop provides neither the evidence nor the errors in logic that might warrant choice of his wage bill model over models using other maximands. Collective rent maximization is dismissed as being "without any discernable counterpart in trade union policies." Unfortunately, he offers no information suggesting that his preferred maximand has such a counterpart in trade union policies.

5. Dunlop, *Wage Determination*, p. 33. The higher the wage rate, the larger the number of workers willing to affiliate with the union.

6. This assumption operates only where the entire workforce is unionized or where union members have first claim on all work opportunities. Of course, unless the union permits nonunion workers to be employed at lower wage rates, this latter condition also implies the complete exclusion of nonunion workers. If *both* conditions are relaxed, the intersection of the membership function and the demand curve provides little information, since the former may include unemployed members and the latter may include nonunion hires. This was first pointed out by Atherton *(Union Bargaining Goals)* in his critique of Dunlop's claim that the wage bill model produced unambiguous results, even where firms were not totally unionized. However, as just mentioned, *both* conditions must be relaxed before ambiguity results.

7. This was, essentially, the maximand put forward by Henry Simons, "Reflections on Syndicalism," p. 8. But wage rates and employment levels that make a minority of members *too* unhappy run the risk of driving away members who might then become competitive. This is a classic cartel problem and is probably what Dunlop had in mind.

8. Atherton was confident that his compensation argument would be one that "economists in particular may be expected to raise." See Atherton, *Union Bargaining Goals*, p. 20.

9. Atherton, *Union Bargaining Goals*, p. 21.

10. The same criticism and counterargument would be advanced by Atherton where the intersection of demand and membership functions is located *above* the unit elastic point. Fifty-one percent of the membership could have a higher income if the wage rate were raised above the intersection and some members lost their jobs.

Compensation would secure employment, in this case, for the entire membership and the wage rate would "return" to the intersection. But see below.

11. Atherton, *Union Bargaining Goals*, p. 21, italics supplied.

12. This implicitly assumes nonprohibitive transaction costs.

13. This point will be developed more fully in chaps. 4, 5, and 6.

14. Even where the membership function is specified, however, as in the case where it describes *all* those who wish to be members at alternative wage rates, we find only ambiguous implications. See Atherton, *Union Bargaining Goals*, pp. 11–12.

15. Although Dunlop discussed some "nonincome objectives of wage policy," such as union policies designed to encourage new members, to allocate work among employees, to acquire nonpecuniary benefits for its members, to control the rate of technological substitution, and to control the entrance of workers to "the" trade, these considerations were never incorporated into the wage bill hypothesis as logical implications of the model. In fact, they could not be logically derived from the wage bill maximand.

16. See Daniel J. B. Mitchell, "Union Wage Policies: The Ross-Dunlop Debate Reopened," *Industrial Relations*, 11 (1972) for a restatement of the controversy and an attempt at synthesis.

17. To my knowledge, only Orley Ashenfelter and George Johnson, "Bargaining Theory, Trade Unions and Industrial Strike Activity," *American Economic Review* 59 (March 1969): 35–49; and Atherton, *Union Bargaining Goals*, have achieved some success along these lines.

18. However, Ross concedes that wage-employment relationships are relatively more decipherable where compensation is based on piece rates, labor cost is a "substantial" part of total cost, the product market is highly competitive, and the given industry or firm is not fully organized (Ross, *Wage Policy*, p. 100).

19. The suggestion of an analogy to the Berle-Means's "separation of ownership from control" thesis should not escape us. See Adolf Berle and Gardner Means, *The Modern Corporation and Private Property* (New York: MacMillan, 1932).

20. There is now a small but potent literature that challenges Berle-Means and develops this point. See Armen A. Alchian and Harold Demsetz, "Production Information Costs and Economic Organization," *American Economic Review* 62 (December 1972); and Michael Jensen and William Meckling, "Theory of the Firm: Managerial Behavior, Agency Costs and Ownership Structure," Journal of Financial Economics (October 1976).

21. Ross does, in fact, mention some constraints that permit the exercise of discretionary behavior by the leadership. " . . . The rank and file are extremely dependent upon the officials for guidance on what is equitable, obtainable, and acceptable as well as for all the indispensable tactical wisdom which only they possess. In consequence, the procedures originally designed to guarantee control by the rank and file have become devices for control of the rank and file," (Ross, *Wage Policy*, p. 44).

22. In addition to possible differences in information cost between the two constituencies, the returns to investment in policing differ between stockholders and union members, because the nature of ownership differs. This distinction will be fundamental to the model presented in chaps. 4 and 5 and to the analysis of union behavior that will distinguish this work from others.

23. See Melvin Reder, "The Theory of Union Wage Policy," *Review of Economics and Statistics*, 34 (February 1952): 34–45 for an excellent critique on this point. A noted exception is the attempt by O. Eckstein and T. Wilson, "The Determination of Money Wages in American Industry," *Quarterly Journal of Economics*, 76

(August 1962): 379–414. The authors sought to explain changes in money wage levels in U.S. manufacturing by use of "equitable comparisons," and "orbits of coercive comparisons."

24. See, however, the reviews by Jan Pen, *Journal of Economic Literature 12, 2* (June 1974): 536–537; and James E. Annable, *Industrial and Labor Relations Review* 28 (October 1974): 166–167.

25. This approach to unions is certainly not new. Both Fellner, *Competition,* and Cart-ter, *Theory of Wages,* use the utility maximand, with wage rates and employment as arguments, for a union's objective function. My criticism of Atherton's work, especially as it applies to his "target zones" discussed below, may be applied to the relevant parts of their work also.

26. Throughout his book, Atherton either assumes firms are totally organized, or that "members" include all those workers who are *potential* members. This sidesteps the important issue of union policy toward nonmembers, which will be discussed in later chapters.

27. Atherton's focus on the "disutility of strike days" ignores the possibility that strikes may provide the average member with some utility enhancing leisure, especially if he may draw on strike benefits and/or unemployment compensation and food stamps. On the other hand, to the extent that strikes imply manning pickets and risking violence or engaging in less valuable, temporary work elsewhere, the utility increments associated with work stoppages of one kind or another are mitigated.

28. Atherton does not attempt to work through the maximization of equations (2.1), (2.1a) and (2.1b) by use of Lagrangian multipliers. Nor are first and second order conditions discussed.

29. The fixed levels of h, t, and p are convenient auxiliary assumptions that make two-dimensional geometric comparisons useful. The functions can accommodate simul-taneous variations in all the components of real income, although the analysis must shift from geometric space to calculus.

30. Since h is held constant, combinations of w and e that maintain a given level of z imply different levels of utility (x) in wage-hour space, not shown. The x scale on the ordinate axis, in fig. 2.1, represents ordinate measures of utility in earnings-employment space. Higher levels of wage-hours imply higher levels of x. However, it should be remembered that differences in x are not measured cardinally.

31. Note that the relationship between W and Z_i is unchanged as strike length is in-creased, other things the same. This is readily seen at \$4.00. More strike days at \$4.00 yield lower levels of U_i while Z remains at Z_4.

32. The formation of union bargaining goals, in this model, is not dramatically altered by the relaxation of homogeneous preferences among the membership. Atherton introduces these differences by assuming that membership-preferences are finite and that members can be arranged into preference groups. Each group has an op-timum wage rate goal determined, as in fig. 2.2, by the tangency between the em-ployers strike-length function and one of the indifference curves reflecting that group's preferences. Weighting each group by its membership, the wage rate goal that can be supported by a majority of weighted groups determines the union's *ma-jority optimum.* However this "optimum" is constrained by the "critical" utility level, below which minority groups will threaten to leave the union or otherwise af-filiate with another collective bargaining unit. See Atherton, *Union Bargaining Goals,* chap. 4, pp. 80–89.

33. So that, in the case of a price level increase, marginal value product and the em-ployer strike function shift up less than in proportion to the consumer price level.

34. A rise in p or t (i.e., a fall in real income), for example, will result in a rise in the

union's wage objective, a rise in its desired strike length, and a fall in its desired level of employment, other things the same.

35. Atherton, *Union Bargaining Goals*, p. 70.

36. The same criticism applies to Cartter's trade union model as well (Cartter, *Theory of Wages*, pp. 90–106.

37. Strictly speaking, this is not the solution Atherton describes, as it does not take into account the strike function that is so important in his model (see fig. 2.2). However, the solution described here is not inconsistent with the Atherton model, even where the strike function is explicitly recognized.

38. The Atherton model does not address the logical possibility of a "no strike optimum," that is, a demand curve-indifference curve tangency, at or below the market clearing wage rate. While this result seems implausible, it is not ruled out by the logical structure of the model.

39. Apparently, Atherton's reason for including the variable (e), employment, in the individual member's utility function was to account for the fact that any given member cannot be certain of his continued employment in the face of a wage increase (Atherton, *Union Bargaining Goals*, pp. 32, 39, and 50). This, however, would require an expected utility approach to the rank and file's decisionmaking process. Since such an approach is ignored by Atherton, except when uncertainty is brought into the leadership's calculus (see his chap. 6), the relevance of (e) in Atherton's basic model should be questioned. This objection notwithstanding, a probability approach to rent maximization, other things the same, would yield different results, in terms of observable wage rates and employment, from the perfect certainty case; i.e., lower wage rates and more employment. In cases other than risk neutrality, expected utility maximization and expected rent maximization would yield different results. See John Moore, "Uncertainty and Sticky-Downward But Upward-Mobile Wages," *Economic Inquiry*, 13, 4 (December 1975); and my discussion in chap. 6.

40. At an earlier point Atherton states, curiously, "Unions seek to maximize, *first*, the probability of union survival and, *second*, the probability of continuation in office of the incumbents" (Atherton, *Union Bargaining Goals*, p. 29). Much later he reiterates these maximands, referring to them as "the union's basic goals, which determine its preferences . . . . " (p. 99, *italics supplied*). Analogously, this interpretation is equivalent to the statement that the firm must first cover its variable costs, i.e., survive, before it can pursue the luxury of maximizing profits.

41. These include costs attendant to collective bargaining and attributable to the administration of the agreement, to legal aid and political action, to record keeping and other internal administration, to entertainment or other recreational programs, and to promotional activities encouraging new memberships and retaining old ones (Atherton, *Union Bargaining Goals*, pp. 72–73).

42. In the limit, the leadership would seek a market-clearing wage rate.

43. If the assumption of identical rank and file preferences is retained, the minimal satisfaction level is the same for all members.

44. Likewise, the employment associated with the institutional optimum will be equal to or greater than the level associated with the membership optimum, but still less than that associated with a market-clearing wage rate.

45. While he is not unalterably wedded to this maximand (e.g., he does mention, at one point, the minimization of employer or governmental antagonism) it is the one that Atherton employs most frequently.

46. Conspicuously absent from the list of costs facing the union (adopted by Atherton, see, *Union Bargaining Goals*, pp. 73–74) for which dues must be generated, are the

leaders' salaries. Moreover, Atherton fails to discuss the connection between leadership remuneration and dues receipts. We are left with only a hint, as quoted, of why we might logically expect net revenue maximizing from leaders.

47. The equivalency of profit and utility maximization for entrepreneurs in private-for-profit firms can be established under fairly reasonable assumptions. See Robert M. Feinberg, "Utility Maximization vs. Profit Maximization," *Southern Economic Journal* 42 (July 1975): 130–132; E. O. Olson, Jr., "Profit Maximization Versus Utility Maximization: A Correction," *Southern Economic Journal*, 43, (January 1977).

48. We abstract from tax-deductible business expenses.

49. Consistent with the first law of demand, less will be chosen at a higher price.

50. See, for example, Armen A. Alchian, "The Basis of Some Recent Advances in The Theory of Management of the Firm," *Journal of Industrial Economics*, 14 (November 1965). Becker, *Economics of Discrimination*, Kenneth W. Clarkson, "Some Implications of Property Rights in Hospital Management," *Journal of Law and Economics*, 15 (October 1972), Louis De Alessi, "An Economic Analysis of Government Ownership and Regulation: Theory and Evidence from the Electric Power Industry," *Public Choice* 14 (Fall 1974); and Harold Demsetz, "Toward a Theory of Property Rights," *American Economic Review*, 57 (May 1967).

51. The firm is faced with continuing market pressure from would-be owners (or in the case of the corporation, nonmanagement owners) to direct resources toward profit maximization.

52. See De Alessi, "Economic Analysis," for a discussion of management tenure under alternative ownership constraints in the electric power industry.

53. However, if net dues revenues are increased by merger with other unions rather than by growth in employment *via* wage rates lower than desired by current members, it would be in the interest of the rank and file to link salaries to net revenues—especially where the latter are used to benefit members. Atherton, however, does not discuss this point.

54. See chap. 2.

55. Of course, if variable costs are unaffected, the rise in average costs merely implies a *diversion* of maximum net revenue to leaders.

56. That is, where a dollar of such revenues taken outside the union is more costly to an officer than a dollar taken inside the union.

57. The threat of rent dissipation and its implications for the structure of union institutions will be discussed below. See Powel, *Theory of Union Behavior*.

58. Apparently, the only wealth-maximizing possibility acknowledged by Dunlop, but quickly excluded from his analysis, is the model of the union "run for the exclusive profit of the organizer" (Dunlop, *Wage Determination* pp. 32–33). For a more rigorous treatment of this model, see Paul A. Weinstein, "Racketeering and Labor: An Economic Analysis," *Industrial and Labor Relations Review* 14 (April 1966). Dunlop rejects this maximand as "without any readily discernible counterpart in trade union policies." But the maximization of the collective rents is not inconsistent with a racketeering model where such rents are appropriated for "the exclusive profit of the organizer."

59. For an earlier model using a wealth maximand, see Sherwin Rosen, "Unionism and Occupational Wage Structure in the United States," *International Economic Review* (June 1970).

60. The supply price may be multidimensional and need not be expressed solely in terms of pecuniary wage rates. This means that monopoly rents can be multidimensional also. At this point, however, and in keeping with the Powel model,

monopoly rents will be determined by the difference between market-clearing and contractual wage rates.

61. But Paul A. Weinstein ("Racketeering and Labor") and Gary S. Becker ("Union Restrictions on Entry," in *The Public Stake in Union Power* [Charlottesville, Va.: University of Virginia Press, 1959]) are notable exceptions.

3. OWNERSHIP PROFILE OF THE TRADE UNION

1. See Robert A. Gorman, *Labor Law, Unionization and Collective Bargaining* (St. Paul: West Publishing Co., 1976), chap. 22. There is now some question as to the breadth of the antitrust exemption after Local 189 Meat Cutters vs. Jewel Tea Co. (U.S. 1965) and Connell Construction Company vs. Plumbers Local 100 (U.S. 1975). For a discussion of the implications of this case, see pp. 631–35.
2. See Gorman, *Labor Law,* pp. 374–381.
3. Section 7 of the National Labor Relations Act (1935) protects workers using concerted activities against an employer from discharge or other relaliation.
4. A challenge to the legitimacy of incumbent representation may not be made within twelve months of a representation election. Otherwise exclusive representation may be insulated from rival petitions for representation elections to the N.L.R.B. for up to three years after the signing of a collective bargaining agreement. See Gorman, *Labor Law,* pp. 54–55.
5. See Labor Management Relations Act, 61 Stat. 136 (1947) as amended by 73 Stat. 519 (1959), 83 Stat. 133 (1969), 87 Stat. 314 (1973), 88 Stat. 396 (1974), 29 U.S.C.
   There is still some uncertainty about the suability of unions over questions of diversity jurisdiction in other than contract violation issues or violations of federal law. These questions arise where the state in which the federal court is located does not recognize unions as independent entities, if the latter are unincorporated associations, or where the state does not permit class action suits on behalf of unincorporated associations. See S.L. Cohn, "Problems in Establishing Federal Jurisdiction Over an Unincorporated Labor Union," *Georgetown Law Journal,* 47 (1959): 492–587.
6. See point 7 below.
7. Joseph R. Grodin, *Union Government and The Law* (Institute of Industrial Relations, University of California at Los Angeles, 1961), pp. 163–165.
8. Ibid., pp. 165–77.
9. See R.K. Evans, "The Law of Agency and the National Union," *Kentucky Law Journal,* 49 (1961): 295–350.
10. See U.S. vs. White, 322 US 694; 152 ALR 1202.
11. See Farrar vs. Messmer, 368 S.W. 2d 933 (Mo.Ap.).
12. See Amer. Jus. 2d, Labor and Labor Relations, Paragraph 190–199.
13. See Grodin, *Union Government,* pp. 150–55.
14. These interests, however, are not totally private, in that the club usually rules on the acceptability of the transfer.
15. This union issued negotiable certificates to its members. Each certificate represented a claim to work opportunity relative to noncertified longshoremen. Any claim owner could sell his share(s) to the highest bidder; it was his private alienable property. See Charles P. Larrowe, *Shape-up and Hiring Hall* (Berkeley and Los Angeles: University of California Press, 1955), p. 88.
16. Several cases have challenged this arrangement. See Phaler vs. Theatrical Protective Union 62 LRRM 2689, 1966.

17. However, this filial transfer system has been found in conflict with state fair employment practice laws, the Taft Hartley Act and the Civil Rights Act of 1964. See Grodin, *Union Government*, pp. 174–81.
18. See Alfred Nicols, "Stock Versus Mutual Savings and Loan Associations: Some Evidence of Differences in Behavior," *American Economic Review*, 57 (May 1967): 337–46.
19. Of course these practices are now outlawed but have not been effectively abolished.
20. See Grodin, *Union Government*, pp. 174–80. Prior to the *LMRDA* some state courts did rule that exclusion from participation was equivalent to exclusion from membership and a violation of the due process clause of the Constitution. See Betts vs. Easley, 161 Kan. 459, 169 P. 2d 1946. See also James vs. Marinship Corp., 25 Cal. 2d 721 155 P. 2d 329 (1944).
21. *LMRDA*, Section 101(a) (1). See Grodin, *Union Government*, p. 180.
22. Plaintiffs are not prevented from seeking redress in state courts where exhaustion requirements may be less inhibiting. But see Grodin, *Union Government*, pp. 48–49.
23. *LMRDA*, Section 101(a) (4). See Grodin, *Union Government*, p. 47.
24. See Nichols, "Stock Versus Mutual Savings and Loan," p. 339.
25. Directory of National Unions and Employee Associations, 1975, Bureau of Labor Statistics Bulletin, 1937.
26. The collective bargaining influence of union activity reaches beyond its membership. In 1974, for example, 1.3 million nonunion workers were covered by collective bargaining contracts, (ibid).
27. Ibid., p. 4.
28. Teamsters, Printing and Graphic, Electrical Workers, Retail Clerks, Operating Engineers, Machinists, Steel Workers, Meat Cutters, and Service Workers.
29. B.L.S. Bulletin, p. 22.
30. Unions and employee associations as a fraction of the labor force declined from 25.2 percent to 24.5 percent between 1968 and 1974. Ibid., p. 63.
31. *Selected Earnings and Demographic Characteristics of Union Members, 1970.* Bureau of Labor Statistics Report 417, 1972, p. 2.
32. Ibid. Comparability criteria are not clear from the B.L.S. report.
33. Ibid., table 2, p. 8.
34. Ibid.
35. Ibid.
36. Ibid.
37. Ibid.

4. THE BASIC MODEL IN PROPRIETARY PARADIGM

1. Reder, "Job Scarcity."
2. To the extent that the union has a comparative advantage in the production of some goods, such as grievance services, contract policing, group purchase benefits, and others, the union itself will be a source of rents to the membership, completely independent of the benefits arising from any monopoly power it may exercise. This, however, should not suggest that rents arising from grievance services, etc., performed by the union, are necessarily independent of that power. In fact, it should not be surprising to find unions with relatively more monopoly power providing relatively better or more services to their membership, cet. par. Nevertheless, this explains why some unions survive even when their monopoly power in the labor market is nil.

3. Where jurisdiction may be defined by occupation, plant, industry, or location.
4. Nor does it include the requirement that employers consult the union before making labor-saving changes in the productive process.
5. Work rules found in the West Coast longshoring industries prior to 1962 are examples of the latter. See Wytze Gorter and G.H. Hildebrand, *The Pacific Coast Maritime Shipping Industry, 1930-1948* (Berkeley and Los Angeles: University of California Press, 1954); and M. D. Kossoris, "Working Rules in West Coast Longshoring," *Monthly Labor Review*, 89 (January 1961): 1-10.
6. Mancur Olson, *The Logic of Collective Action*, Harvard University Press, Cambridge, Mass:, 1965, chap. 3. Union managers play an important role here also. See chap. 6 below. See, also, H. Gregg Lewis, "Competitive and Monopoly Unionism," in *The Public Stake in Union Power*, ed. Philip D. Bradley (Charlottesville, Va.: University Press of Virginia, 1959), pp. 181-208.
7. Selig Perlman, *A Theory of the Labor Movement*, 1928 (Reissued New York: Augustus M. Kelley, 1949), p. 269.
8. Although this is illegal under the Taft-Hartley Act, a union with sufficient monopoly power can convince the firm that the expected value cost of a Taft-Hartley violation will be smaller than the cost of union action if the worker isn't somehow let go. See, for example: Beauchamp *vs.* Weeks, 2 Lab. Rel. Rep. (48 L.R.R.M.) 3048 (S.D. Cal. September 27, 1961).
9. It is interesting to note that Perlman, *A Theory of Labor Movement*, cites the closed shop as an innovation designed "as much to . . . 'conserve' the jobs as to make the bargaining solidarity with the employer *treason proof.*" See p. 269. Italics supplied.
10. Although the closed shop would appear to offer greater benefits to unions than the union shop, there is some evidence that even prior to the Taft-Hartley Act of 1948 some unions actively sought the latter institution. These were mainly the industrial unions. We conjecture that the heterogeneity of occupations and skills found in the firms and industries that industrial unions sought to organize made employers particularly resistant to the closed shop. That is, although skill levels in these industries may have been relatively low, and thus preemployment screening errors relatively inexpensive, the great variety of skills to be coordinated required a broader perspective than closed shop unions could be "trusted" to pursue. Moreover, because the employer-employee relationship in these industries was usually less casual than in craft industries, it was less costly (to unions) to monitor individual arrangements between employer and worker and thus there was less incentive, from the union's perspective, to seek preemployment screening devices such as those offered by the closed shop.
11. The model discussed in this section owes much inspiration to Kenneth Clarkson, "Organizational Constraints and Models of Managerial Behavior," in *The Economics of Nonproprietary Institutions*, ed. Kenneth W. Clarkson and Donald L. Martin, Greenwich, Conn.: J.A.I. Press, 1980.
12. The notion that union monopoly rents include nonpecuniary elements is not novel. Earlier, Becker (*Union Restrictions on Entry*, p. 209) noted that "Most economists would agree that union power has been imperfectly estimated partly because the measure ignores union effects on *nonpecuniary* and *future income* . . . " (Italics supplied.) Moreover, empirical examination of the relationship between wage and nonwage supplements led Robert Rice ("Skill, Earnings and The Growth of Wage Supplements," *American Economic Review*, May 1966, p. 592) to conclude that "relative money wage differentials progressively understate differentials in compensation, as measured by the sum of money earnings plus wage supplement expenditures . . . it is clear that we should not examine money wage differentials assuming that private wage supplements are proportional to total wages."

13. Although rare in the industrial relations literature, economists have employed the notion that unions produce monopoly rents for their members in order to explain phenomena such as the occupational wage structure and union dues differentials. See Rosen, "Unionism and Occupational Wage Structure," and John Powel, "A Theory of Union Behavior."

14. $\bar{W}$ $(\overline{mH})/P^*$ and $\hat{W}$ $(\overline{mH})/P^*$ are real disposable claims on general purchasing power and may also be expressed in (1) in terms of discounted market values of goods that members will consume, (P_oG_o) and $(P_o^!G_o^!)$, respectively. This notation, under certain assumptions, will be used interchangeably with $\bar{W}$ $(\overline{mH})$ at a later point when discussing variations in $\bar{W}$.

15. Depending upon the composition of remuneration per man-hour, wage elasticity in unionized industries may undertake true labor cost elasticity and appear less stable than the latter.

16. Given equations (1) and (2), maximization of ϱ_T, the present value of union job rights or member wealth, requires that for each input employed by the union:

$$\frac{d\varrho_T}{dx_i} = 0 = (mH) + W \frac{\partial\ (mH)}{\partial W} \frac{\partial W}{\partial x_i} + P,\ G_1 \frac{\partial G_1}{\partial x_i} = F + X \frac{\partial F}{\partial X} \frac{\partial X}{\partial x_i}$$

This is merely the condition that the sum of the marginal revenue products of a given input, as it is applied to the production of various union outputs, must equal the marginal factor cost of that input if total rent is to be maximized. This particular formulation allows for the effect unions may have on man-hours employed and the prices of nonwage payments G_1. Note that some G_1 goods may be jointly or collectively consumed by members and no per unit transfer price may be associated with them. As in the conventional analysis of the firm, the maximization of rent by the union also requires that for any two inputs:

$$\frac{dx_j}{dx_i} = \frac{\Sigma\ MVPx_i}{\Sigma\ MVPx_j} = \left[\frac{F + X\partial F/\partial X}{F + X\partial F/\partial x}\right]\ \partial x_i//\partial X - \partial x_j$$

17. One of the few published empirical applications of a union rent-maximizing theory to union wage differentials is presented in Rosen, "Unionism and Occupational Wage Structure."

18. Note again that so long as the members' utility is affected by job related environmental characteristics, the negotiability of job rights offers no guarantee that members will have tastes consistent with rent maximization. It does, however, suggest that in this case tastes are more likely to be coincident with rent maximizing than where job rights are not transferable. See Robert A. Fienberg, "Utility Maximization"; E. O. Olson, Jr., "Profit Maximization Versus Utility Maximization: A Correction;" and footnote 19.

19. Since member preferences, for purposes of simplicity, are identical, there is a strong temptation to use an aggregate utility function to describe the "union" and its bargaining goals. This temptation is resisted here, if only because we will soon be discussing situations where member interests diverge and we wish to avoid the impression, so often advanced by earlier writers, that the union is some entity *outside* the individual preferences of *all* those who compose its membership and chart its policy. See, for example, Cartter, *Theory of Wages*.

20. This particular formulation calls attention to what should be obvious, that persons do not bargain for wages *qua* wages, but for the utility associated with the market basket of goods money wages may purchase.

21. The effect of changes in P* on W̄ will be discussed.
22. The following constraint is formulated in terms of "proprietary unionism." That is, members may capture *and transfer* their weighted share of the *full capitalized value* of any rents produced by the union. A more general constraint on member utility maximizing behavior is presented in the next chapter.
23. The more senior the card holder, *cet. par.*, the lower is θ.
24. Second order conditions in G_o and G_1 are:

$$d^2\phi/dG_o^2 = \theta \, \partial^2 U/\partial G_o^2 + \lambda \, \partial^2 \varrho_m/\partial G_o^2 < 0 \qquad (5.6)$$

$$d^2\phi/dg_j^2 = \theta \, \partial^2 U/\partial g_j^2 + \lambda \, \partial^2 \varrho_m/\partial g_j^2 < 0 \qquad (5.7)$$

25. It should immediately be objected that a wage increase will reduce employment for someone and that this fact destroys the collective good analogy. But the employment effects of a wage hike need not result in disemployment for incumbent workers. A common response to the higher cost of labor is employment cutbacks through attrition. Thus, it is not unreasonable to assume that incumbent members, individually, view increased wage rates as a collective good.
26. Although not commonly treated as a union, some fundamental similarities between conventional unions and the Exchange were recognized rather early. See John Mitchell, *Organized Labor*, Philadelphia American Book and Bible House, 1903, (chap. 2), p. 210. Until they were recently determined a violation of antitrust legislation, brokerage fees were fixed by collective action to avoid competition between sellers of brokerage services. In addition to the capital value of a seat on the Exchange, members also pay dues, charges, fines and other assessments as determined by the board of directors and authorized by the Exchange's constitution. Moreover, the board has the authority to maintain the market value of seats by purchasing and holding an amount sufficient to achieve that end. Thus, entry into the Exchange is restricted, the terms of trade have been fixed by the collective and collusive power of the membership, and members are assessed to support the operations of collusive activities.
27. Members enjoy something less than full private-property rights in their status. The sale of a seat must be to an American citizen at least 21 years of age. Moreover, the would-be buyer must be sponsored by two incumbent members of at least one year's standing who know the applicant personally and will endorse his conduct. The candidate must also furnish three letters of recommendation and a detailed description of his business history. He submits to a complete medical examination at the Exchange and passes a written examination of his knowledge of the Exchange's function and operations. Several financing arrangements for the purchase of seats are authorized but in no case may financing exceed three years. See New York Stock Exchange Inc. Constitution and Rules (1976).
28. Katrina V. Berman, *Worker Owned Plywood Companies*, Seattle: Washington State University Press. I am grateful to Evsy Domar for suggesting this example of proprietary unionism.
29. See Charles P. Larrowe, *Shape-Up*, p. 88.
30. See Donald L. Martin, "Job Property Rights and Job Defections," *Journal of Law and Economics* 15 (October 1972).
31. Given our ownership assumptions, this conclusion is not so obvious once the identical tastes assumption is relaxed.
32. See Olson, *The Logic of Collective Action*, chap. 1, pp. 22-33 and chap. 3. Olson demonstrates, formally, that small groups are capable of voluntarily producing collective goods and that their output is likely to be suboptimal unless other auxiliary rationing devices are adopted.

33. These conditions have been set out by Hicks in his *Theory of Wages*, (London: St. Martins Press, 1964), pp. 241–246. Briefly, relatively small groups of labor can affect relatively low labor demand elasticities where the elasticity of substitution between that group and other factors of production is smaller than the price elasticity of the final product, and where the elasticity of supply of cooperating factors is also "low." On the other hand, relatively small groups of labor will find it more difficult to raise wages effectively if the elasticity of substitution is *larger* than the price elasticity of demand for the final product, ceteris paribus. The latter set of conditions would yield lower elasticities of labor demand the *larger* the group engaging in collective action. Since larger groups are more difficult to organize, on a voluntary basis, it is not surprising that mass production industries with large numbers of employees, such as automobiles and steel, had to wait until legislation gave unions a mechanism to make collective bargaining apply universally within a firm or industry. This mechanism, of course, is the Wagner Act, which required firms to recognize a union as exclusive bargaining agent for *all* of its employees (within a designated bargaining unit) if a majority of workers voted for it. The act also legalized both closed and union shops. Although all unions might be expected to welcome compulsory unionism as a means of monitoring free-rider problems, among other things, it was particularly welcomed in those firms where successful collective action required the organization of large numbers of workers, because the elasticity of substitution of capital for labor was greater than the elasticity of final product demand.

34. The diagram is adopted from Lewis, "Competitive and Monopoly Unionism."

35. Without entry restriction or some other rationing device, more than L* − M* nonmembers would seek to share rents also. The extra quantity supplied would result in a dissipation of all rents, including those sought by M*. This suggests that the union would be willing to devote up to the value of rents they expect to claim, under restricted entry, in order to keep out surplus workers. See footnote 36 for an explanation of entry restriction.

36. Entry restriction may take the forms of licensing statutes (as in the case of barbers, plumbers, electricians, and physicians), schooling requirements, or years of experience (statutory or collectively bargained) and the closed shop. Although the licensing statutes are usually achieved through legislation and thus require lobbying costs, policing costs are borne by taxpayers. The closed shop, on the other hand, is a collective bargaining item that the union has to win through negotiation or strike and then has to police at its own expense. Although formally outlawed, less explicit variants of this arrangement are not uncommon. To the extent that unions bargain for the de facto right to reject new workers for cause under a union shop agreement, the effect is a closed shop. Thus, some forms of restriction may be cheaper than others. See Powel, "Theory of Union Behavior." This treatment of the closed shop should not suggest that its sole purpose is to limit market entry or the supply of labor to firms. It was mainly used to extract rents from new workers demanded by firms and applied by the union, and to police or monitor union member behavior.

37. These arrangements appear to suggest that at least some members will not receive as much work at W* as they wish, and that moonlighting may be prevalent. This result depends upon the relationship between the costs of switching between two jobs and the costs of buying off excess workers (i.e., beyond L*) with early retirements, subsidized search and relocation to other firms, etc., so that *active* membership approximates L*. On the other hand, membership need not be limited (nor anyone's demand for work left unsatisfied in any dimension) if the union intro-

duces, at some rent-dissipating cost, work rules and featherbedding, as has been practiced in the railroad and longshoring industries.

38. Where initial membership is greater than L*, the rent maximization hypothesis is not sufficient to predict optimal membership size without information about differences between job rationing costs and the transaction costs associated with buying out "excess" members.

39. This implication was first suggested by Powel, "Theory of Union Behavior," but his otherwise excellent analysis is marred by a failure to derive his rent-maximizing model from the clearly nonproprietary assumptions he makes concerning the ownership characteristics of unions. See especially his chap. 2, p. 11.

40. This point seems to have been ignored by a number of writers. See, for example, Henry Simons, "Reflections on Syndicalism," pp. 131–32, and Charles Lindblom, *Unions and Capitalism,* pp. 30–39. However, confiscatory policies are not inconsistent with wealth maximization where they are applied to a subset of firms in a collective agreement to the beneift of other firms in the agreement. See Oliver Williamson, "Wage Rates as a Barrier to Entry: The Pennington Case in Perspective," *Quarterly Journal of Economics,* 82 (February, 1968), pp. 123–138.

41. Transitory demand shifts may be too costly for unions to ration by higher wage rates, given the cost of collective bargaining. Alternatively, some additional rents may be captured by the sale of temporary work permits. This point is discussed below.

42. Reder, "Job Scarcity," pp. 350–51. Italics supplied.

43. Where entry restriction costs are higher than the costs of monitoring job assignment schemes, such as work sharing, union preference rules, etc., increases in demand may cause membership to expand beyond $\hat{L}(\hat{M})$.

44. We assume here that over certain ranges the employment effects of wage rate changes occur through attrition.

45. Chap. 2, above.

46. The pricing of new memberships under proprietary and nonproprietary assumptions is the subject of chap. 6.

47. Moore, "Uncertainty," p. 599.

48. Ibid., p. 560.

49. By extension, there must be even more rent distributions that would satisfy only a majority of members.

50. Following Moore, this implicitly abstracts from questions of risk preference, although he does discuss this issue at a later point.

51. See chap. 5 of this book.

52. See Robert Lucas and Leonard Rapping, "Real Wages, Employment, and Inflation," *Journal of Political Economy* 77, no. 5, September 1969, pp. 721–54; and Orley Ashenfelter, George Johnson, and John Pencavel, "American Trade Union Growth: 1900–1960." *Quarterly Journal of Economics* 83 (August 1969): 434–48.

53. Atherton, *Union Bargaining Goals,* pp. 59–70.

54. Ibid., p. 59. See my discussion of the strike-length function in chap. 2.

55. Ibid.

56. A price level increase raises p_j and lowers ϱ_m, in the numerator of (6′) resulting in a *rise* in the effective price, $(p_j - \dfrac{\partial \varrho_m}{\partial g_j})$, of the *private* good.

57. See Ashenfelter, Johnson, and Pencavel, "American Trade Union Growth."

58. However, see Feinberg, "Utility Maximization."

59. Since the transaction costs of side payments can affect rent-maximizing opportunities, the functional relationship between such costs and the size of membership may represent a constraint on the size of proprietary unions.

5. THE NONPROPRIETARY UNION

1. Filial preference appears to be illegal under the Civil Rights Act of 1964. See Phalen v. Theatrical Protective Union, 62 LRRM 2689.

2. Aside from the explicit proprietary arrangements in union cards ascribed to Seattle longshore unions at the turn of the century (Larrowe, *Shape-Up*), markets for union cards have been clandestine and apparently infrequent. See Donald L. Martin, "Job Property Rights and Job Defections," *Journal of Law and Economics* 15 (October 1972); idem, "Some Economics of Job Property Rights in The Longshore Industry," *The Journal of Economics and Business* (Winter) 1973. We have already mentioned that proprietary arrangements in unionlike organizations (e.g., the New York Stock Exchange and the Pacific Coast Plywood Industries) do exist but are also rare.

3. Where there is no heir, the card usually reverts to the union, to be awarded by a majority vote or some other criterion. See Martin, "Job Property Rights."

4. A third, perhaps less important, explanation for the absence of proprietary institutions in trade unions concerns the pecuniary conflict between any individual member and the collection of members where there exist private-property rights in membership cards. For example, a retiring member, or one who is leaving the union's jurisdiction, would be interested in capturing at least some of the rents he would have received had he stayed on. Sale of his card to a newly hired worker would achieve this. Alternatively, if the new worker were issued a *new* card instead, rents would be extracted from him through initiation fees, dues, and wage differentials in which the remaining members could participate, however modestly. This suggests that unless incumbent members can be compensated for each and every transaction involving the transfer of membership status from an existing member to a would-be member, alienability in union cards will be resisted by the great majority of the membership.

5. Although not stated explicitly, the assumed value of α in the proprietary model of chap. 4 was unity.

6. This last case suggests the plight of rank and file members of a "racketeering" union making "sweetheart" contracts with employers. *Effective* wage rates to union members are no greater than levels determined by competitive forces. See Weinstein ("Racketeering and Labor").

7. Jensen and Meckling, in an important paper concerning ownership and control questions in the theory of the firm, use the notation α to identify the fraction of shares owned by managers in order to derive implications about managerial discretion. Although the use of α in this and the next chapter is analogous to Jensen-Meckling, it was developed completely independent of their effort and before publication of their article. (Michael Jensen and William Meckling, "Theory of the Firm: Managerial Behavior, Agency Costs and Ownership Structure," *Journal of Financial Economics*, 3 (October 1976).

8. The second-order condition in the g_jth good is

$$\frac{d^2\phi}{dg_j^2} = \frac{\theta \, \partial^2 U}{\partial g_j^2} + \lambda \frac{(\alpha \, \partial^2{}_m)}{\partial g_j^2} > 0 \qquad (5.7')$$

9. Wage receipts, of course, may be exchanged in the marketplace for *transferable* claims on future consumption. Strictly speaking, a value of α less than 1 makes current pecuniary *and* nonpecuniary sources of rent relatively less expensive.

10. However, the threat of picketing and strikes is ever present.

11. See Bureau of Labor Statistics Bulletin 1905, p. 180. This episode was first brought to my attention in a paper by Levis A. Kochin, "The Social Cost of Union Monopoly," University of Washington Department of Economics (unpublished), p. 8.

12. Ibid.
13. See Loren M. Solnick and Gerome M. Staller, "The Effect of Unionism on Employer Fringe Benefit Expenditures" (paper presented at the Labor Union Session of the Western Economic Association Meetings, June 26, 1976, San Francisco, California).
14. Ibid., p. 16. Italics supplied.
15. The maximum wage increment foregone constitutes the price to incumbents, p_i of generating rent transfers from membership sales made possible through employment expansion. Of course, beyond some point an additional membership acquired through employment expansion will reduce rents for incumbent members relative to raising the wage rate. Thus, as long as p_i is less than the increment in rent from new memberships, incumbent members will support a wage increase less than the maximum.
16. These symmetrical results were derived in more detail in chap. 4.
17. This implication has been wrongly attributed to a wealth maximizing union, *supra* chap. 4, n. 42.
18. See Reder, "Job Scarcity."
19. In the coal industry it is common to tax tonnage mined to support retirement pensions. To the extent that collective bargaining could have increased current wage rates instead, this practice represents a transfer from all other workers to older workers and again constitutes rent extraction. Likewise, the agreement between the International Longshoremens' and Warehousemens' Union and the Pacific Maritime Association, in the 1960s, concerning payments to the union for the abolition of featherbedding procedures in the longshore industry, involved a transfer of rents from younger to older workers in the form of early retirement benefits. Finally, collective agreements with the Airline Pilots Association link wage rate with the weight of the aircraft. The more experienced and tenured members, of course, fly the larger planes.
20. See supra chap. 4, note 13.
21. There appears to be some controversy in the literature concerning the effect of unionism on wage dispersion among skilled and unskilled workers. Cohen (1967), Weiss (1966), and Goldner (1958) have studied the effects of unionism on the wages of low skilled workers and high skilled workers. Collective bargaining activity appears to raise the wages of the former group relatively more than the latter group, thus narrowing wage dispersion between low skilled and high skilled workers. On the other hand, Rosen (1970), has found that unionism operates to benefit unionized skilled craftsmen relative to all other unionized workers, unless the latter category is disaggregated into semiskilled and unskilled workers. Disaggregation reveals that unskilled laborers gain relatively more than either semiskilled operatives or skilled craftsmen. However, these results challenge the proposition that wage differentials transfer rents from newer to incumbent members, only where incumbents are identified with skilled laborers. Clearly, nothing prevents the ranks of incumbent members from being populated by some unskilled laborers, nor the ranks of newer members from being populated by some skilled craftsmen.
    A recent study by Neumann and Heckman supports the view that rents are ultimately transferred from newer to more tenured members once differences in employment variation between the two groups are considered. Newer members experience more variable employment than incumbent members and this results in some rents being transferred from the former to the latter group. See George Neumann and James Heckman, "Union Wage Differentials and the Decision to Join Unions," University of Chicago, 1977 (unpublished). A more recent paper by J. L. Medoff, "Layoffs and Alternatives Under Trade Unionism in U.S. Manufacturing," *American Economic Review* 69 (June 1979) also identifies differences in

employment variability of union members by tenure and supports the hypothesis that rents are transferred to incumbents via layoff priorities.

22. A detailed discussion and analysis of this role is the subject matter of chap. 6.

23. See Taft (Structure and Government), pp. 105–116. However, some effort to compare union officers' performance with salaries was undertaken by Ehrenberg and Goldner ("Officer Performance and Compensation"). They found evidence for the hypothesis that local union officer salaries were positively related to the ratio of member wage rates to national average wage rates for the same craft.

24. A discussion of some of these constitutional rules is found in chap. 6.

25. The preceding analysis does not suggest, however, that union managers seek to *maximize* either membership or the net revenue arising from essentially fixed initiation fees, dues, and other assessments per worker. The objective function of a leader in a nonproprietary union is discussed in chap. 6.

26. See Moore ("Uncertainty") and the discussion of his model in chap. 4, above.

27. Moore, "Uncertainty."

28. A West Coast longshoremen's union, ILWU, has used a union-nonunion layoff system, while other unions use journeymen-apprentice or "regular men-temporary men" and other such distinctions. See also Medoff, "Layoffs and Alternatives Under Trade Unionism."

29. Where collective agreements contain remuneration *in kind*, the real value of rents will not fall by as much as the price level rises.

30. Since the market price of the collective good is zero, its effective price falls relative to the effective price of private goods.

31. Most unions may be characterized as relatively nonproprietary and it is interesting to note that less than 25 percent of unionized workers are covered by escalator clauses in their contracts. See Beal, Edwin, F. and Edward D. Wickersham, *The Practice of Collective Bargaining*, Homewood, Ill., Irwin Publishing Co., 1959, p. 426.

32. Of course, the more bargaining experiences the same two protagonists have with each other the more information each has about the behavior of the other and the greater the likelihood that subjective probabilities will converge, thus avoiding strikes.

33. For a recent example of such models, see Ashenfelter and Johnson ("Bargaining Theory").

34. The word assessment is defined to include a variety of forms of financing strikes.

35. This point should be kept distinct from any common pool—free rider—implications that derive from a collective strike fund.

36. A National Industrial Conference Board survey of the constitutions of 194 national unions, representing over 17 million union members, revealed that in 53 percent of these organizations, representing over 10 million workers, two-stage strike authorizations were required before strike benefits would be distributed. See *Handbook of Union Government Structure and Procedures NICB* Studies in Personnel Policy No. 150, (no date).

37. Ashenfelter and Johnson ("Bargaining Theory"), p. 36.

38. " . . . Although contrary to the membership's best interests." Ibid., p. 37. The leadership in the A/J model is said to promote strikes in order to inflate underestimates by the rank and file of employers' resistance to wage demands, an alternative to securing agreements for lower increases without a consensus. Although the A/J model makes much of this point, it is difficult to see how leadership may be separated from membership, given their assumptions. To the extent that the latter

must approve strikes by vote, strike calls are clearly expressions of the membership. If a strike can be called without a vote, it still requires the acquiescence of the membership; otherwise, the leaders in the A/J model will ultimately face political retribution. Thus, as contracts expire, holdouts for unrealistic or unreasonable demands reflect a willingness by the rank and file to mount the strike. Although the leadership may have a different estimate of the ultimate outcome from strike activity, however, it doesn't follow that a strike may be foisted upon the membership for its own good, as if it were helpless. Unfortunately, A/J failed to note the conditions that would grant union managers the kind of discretion and insulation from rank and file retribution that A/J claim for their model.

39. Ibid.
40. Ibid., p. 37.
41. The analysis of nonproprietary unions suggests that leaders will discourage rather than promote strike calls, especially those that place a *net* drain on union assets. See chap. 6.

6. MANAGERIAL DISCRETION WITHIN THE UNION

1. For an interesting analysis of membership as an asset, see John Pencavel, "The Demand for Union Services: An Exercise," *Industrial Labor Relations Review*, January 1971, pp. 180–90.
2. To my knowledge, Ross was the first to discuss the analogy between shareholders and union cardholders. See Arthur Ross, *Trade Union Wage Policy* (Berkeley and Los Angeles: University of California Press, 1956), p. 7 and *supra* chap. 1.
3. Although they did not devote much space to labor unions, the present analysis owes much to Armen A. Alchian and Harold Demsetz, "Production Information Costs and Economic Organization," *American Economic Review*, 62 (December 1972): 777–95; and Jensen and Meckling, "Theory of the Firm." With respect to the union case, productivity refers not to members' performance in the workplace, but to their contribution to the production of monopoly rents. This is one of the important characteristics of what Alchian and Demsetz call *team production*, a form of production in which output is larger if several people *cooperate* in completing a task rather than each working separately. By this definition, collective bargaining, strikes and picketing activities to achieve wages above market-clearing levels are team production efforts.
4. Recently, the monitoring function of managerial services has been awarded special prominence in attempts to construct a general theory of organizational behavior, as contrasted with market behavior (Alchian and Demsetz, "Production Information Costs"). With regard to union-type organizations, " . . . some forms of employer performance [other than the payment of money wages] are less easy to meter and are more subject to employer shirking. Fringe benefits often are in nonpecuniary, contingent form; medical, hospital, and accident insurance . . . are contingent payments or performances partly in *kind* by employers to employees. [Rather than] . . . 'trust' the employer not to shirk . . . [employees] would prefer an effective and economic monitor of those payments. We see a specialist monitor—the union employee's agent—hired by them to monitor aspects of employer payments most difficult for the employees to monitor" (ibid., p. 520).
5. As discussed earlier (chap. 4), some union institutions, like the closed and union

shops, are designed partly to police competition among union members. Although Alchian and Demsetz do not discuss this point, the production of monopoly rents by the collective efforts of the membership is a team production effort. Members who are competing away some of these rents by accepting clandestine wage cuts, by breaking restrictive work rules, or by withholding strike and picketing services, are engaging in *shirking*. The larger is the team, the more costly it is for any one member to take offsetting action, and the less expensive it is for any one member to shirk. See also Philip Taft, *The Structure and Government of Labor Unions* (Cambridge: Harvard University Press, 1956), p. 123.

6. Alchian and Demsetz, "Production Information Costs," p. 508.

7. Ibid.

8. Except for the last two, Atherton (*Union Bargaining Goals*) discusses the logical consequences of each of these factors on the behavior of managers.

9. This is not to suggest that nontransferability is an undesirable feature of union membership. As discussed earlier, this rule may be perfectly rational and a net benefit for the union membership as a whole. Moreover, the above statement should not be construed to mean that management can't be voted out of office. A majority of members can accomplish this feat, if they can be persuaded to vote the same way. However, it may be more costly to accomplish this than to purchase additional voting rights.

10. Attributed to a Teamsters Union member referring to former leader Jimmy Hoffa. See John R. Hutchinson, "The Anatomy of Corruption in Trade Unions," *Industrial Relations* 8, no. 2 (1969), p. 141.

11. For an excellent discussion of the expected limits on managerial discretion in proprietary firms with widely dispersed ownership and competitive markets for management, see Alchian, "Corporate Management and Property Rights."

12. Before the Landrum Griffin Act (1959), incumbent officers could and did deny space in union publications and access to membership lists to candidates for union office.

13. This point seems to have been ignored by some earlier scholars. "Unions, even where the level of democratic life is low, are not less responsive to the will of their membership than corporations are to the desires of stockholders." See Taft (1956), p. 35. Taft's point is that the absence of opposition in union elections can be misinterpreted unless the difference between a labor union and other kinds of social organizations is recognized. This difference, he says, is based on the "need" for unions to present a united front to employers and members alike. Although this "need" may be obvious with respect to the former group, it is interesting to dwell upon Taft's explanation regarding the membership. "How are unpalatable compromises to be made and how are contracts, some of whose terms may not be attractive to the union membership, to be enforced when the intelligence or integrity of the leaders are questioned?" (p. 35). Clearly, there is a double entendre here, unless, of course, it is assumed that the leadership of unions, as compared with other social organizations, is infallible. With relatively fewer avenues open to would-be managers in unions, as opposed to corporations, it seems particularly useful to examine the frequency of contested elections as a check on managerial discretion. Taft reports evidence that elections of union officers often go uncontested and that there is a tendency for contests for office to decline over time, suggesting that incumbents are able to build up barriers to competition. See Taft, *Structure and Government of Labor Unions.* pp. 36–64.

14. Ibid., p. 36 and pp. 124–25.

15. Seidman, in Marten Estey, Philip Taft and Martin Wagner, *Regulating Union Government* (New York: Harper and Row, 1964), p. 15.

16. Where size is measured by numbers of voting rights outstanding (i.e., union cards or corporate voting shares).

17. Such threats may manifest themselves through the generation of rival candidates for political office, contests for exclusive bargaining rights promoted by raiding unions, or referendums to discertify the existing union in favor of no union at all. If the assumption of identical rank and file preferences is retained, the nominal level of membership satisfaction consistent with the survival of existing management is identical for all members. Where heterogeneous preferences obtain, the minimal level relevant to survival is determined by the median member-voter. See Atherton (*Union Bargaining Goals*).

18. See National Industrial Conference Board, *Handbook of Union Government Structure and Procedure* (no date).

19. See Elizabeth K. Allison, "Financial Analysis of the Local Union," *Industrial Relations* 14, 2 (May 1975) and Nathan Belfer, "Trade Union Investment Policies," *Industrial and Labor Relations Review* 6, no. 3 (April 1954).

20. This point, to my knowledge, was first made by Clarkson, "Property Rights in Hospital Management," albeit in a nonunion context.

21. This is essentially the experience of the United Farm Workers, the Teamsters Union, and Gallo Brothers, Inc., in California. Farm labor was not covered under the NLRA and so no provision was made for representation elections in this industry. Recently, legislation was enacted in California, with the support of Gallo and both unions, that established voting procedures for representational contests.

22. See David L. Cole, "Interrelationships in The Settlement of Jurisdictional Disputes," *Labor Law Journal* 10 (July 1959): 459-60. Also Joseph Krislov, "The Extent of Trends of Raiding Among American Unions," *Quarterly Journal of Economics*, 69 (February 1955): 152.

23. Cole, "Interrelationships," p. 457.

24. Joseph Krislov, "Raiding Among The Legitimate Unions," *Industrial and Labor Relations Review*, 8, no. 1 (October 1954), p. 28.

25. At most 24 percent in 1950. See Krislov ("Trends of Raiding"), p. 148.

26. Some leaders have been typed *charismatic*, i.e., "[leading] in a creative, imaginative way. By temperament he seeks the new because it is new and minimizes the old because it is old . . . He is public-relations-minded and thinks in terms of plan and program," (see Barbash, 1959, p 488). Others have been typed *operators*, ". . . conscious of what is required to remain in power and of the methods and tactics through which this is achieved" (pp. 490-91). There is also the *administrative leader*. "The impulse of the . . . union leader to act on his own power is further diminished . . . in the 'administrative' leader," (p. 492, italics supplied). Finally, there is *collective leadership*, "Joint consent and participation of the leadership *group* is the dominant leadership characteristic here," (p. 493). See also Mac-Donald, 1959.

27. Where membership preferences are heterogeneous, the utility function of the leader may be identical to the utility function of the median voter, yet behavior of leaders and members need not be identical.

28. For students of union behavior, this appears to be a subtle point. Even Ross (*Trade Union Wage Policy*), who repeatedly recognizes that constraints affect the behavior of leaders (see pp. 27, 30, 31), couches much of his discussion of leadership goals in terms of "the *instinct* for survival and the *impulse* toward growth" (p. 26). Italics supplied.

29. See Alchian, "Corporate Management and Property Rights" in *Economic Policy and the Regulation of Corporate Securities*, 1969, American Enterprise Institute, p. 343.

30. See Leonard Sayles and George Strauss, *The Local Union* (New York: Harcourt, Brace and World, 1967). Leaders of small union locals are more likely to receive most of their income from employment under collective contract than leaders in other organizations. See also Taft (*Structure and Government of Labor Unions*), pp. 98–102. Note that there is some correlation between the salaries of local union business agents and their performance in terms of wage increments. See Ronald Ehrenberg and Steven Goldberg, "Officer Performance and Compensation in Local Building Trade Unions," *Industrial and Labor Relations Review* 30, no. 3 (January 1977): 188–96.

31. This was also recognized by Ross (*Trade Union Wage Policy*), p. 41.

32. See Marten Estey, The Unions: *Structure, Development, and Management* (New York: Harcourt, Brace & World, 1967).

33. Returning to panel C, the median-voter member would be indifferent to payment ratios c'' and c' if he were given a lump sum payment sufficient to place him on utility level $U'U'$ at c'. Thus, where monitoring costs are greater than the improvement in member welfare that would result from policing leaders, the latter may exercise full discretion in bargaining for a payment ratio that would leave the union member at c''.

34. Some evidence supporting this implication is revealed in G.S. Goldstein and M.V. Pauly, "Group Health Insurance as a Local Public Good," in Richard Rosett, *The Role of Health Insurance in The Health Services Sector* (New York: National Bureau of Economic Research, 1976), chap. 3; Solnick (1976); and Rice, "Skill, Earnings, and Growth." Earlier writers noted a tendency for union negotiators to favor benefit plans more strongly than rank and file members. See Mark Greene, *The Role of Employee Benefit Structures in Manufacturing Industry* (University of Oregon Press, 1964), pp. 7–8; and A.I. Mendelsohn, "Fringe Benefits Today and Tomorrow" *Labor Law Journal*, June 1956, pp. 325–328 and 379–384. Researchers that have found worker preferences for benefit increases over money wage increases stronger among union members than among nonunion members, have failed to hold money incomes constant and failed to account for both price level and income tax effects. See Richard A. Lester, "Benefits as a Preferred Form of Compensation," *Southern Economic Journal* 33 (April 1967), pp. 492–94.

35. See chap. 5.

36. See chap. 5.

37. See Reder, "Job Scarcity."

38. See Taft, *Structure and Government of Labor Unions*, pp. 105–16.

39. Ehrenberg and Goldberg, "Officer Performance and Compensation," produced some evidence that local union business agents in the building trades were rewarded for their performance in raising *wage rates* relative to national union/nonunion differentials in the same trade.

40. This also suggests that leaders will be less inclined to favor racial and other discriminatory entrance requirements.

41. See Ross *Trade Union Wage Policy* for the standard argument.

42. In a study of 194 unions covering a declared membership of 17,514,000 individuals, only 16 percent of the unions (15 percent of covered workers) required ratification of collective agreements by the membership. See National Industrial Conference Board, *Handbook of Union Government Structure and Procedures* (1965), p. 51.

43. That level is identical for all in the case of a homogeneous membership and equal to the level of the median voter in a heterogeneous world.

44. These are known as Globe elections and were legitimized in *Globe Machine and Stamping Company*, 3 NLRB 294 (1937).

45. This has been the experience of the International Typographical Union. See Seymour Lipset, Martin Trow, and James Coleman, *Union Democracy: The Internal Politics of The International Typographical Union* (Glencoe, Illinois: Free Press, 1956), pp. 298–301. Also see Atherton, *Union Bargaining Goals*, pp. 95–96.
46. Senate Select Committee on Improper Practices in the Labor or Management Field.
47. See Ross *Trade Union Wage Policy*, p. 93.
48. For example, as part of his "mutual trusteeship" philosophy of unionism, David McDonald, when president of the United Steelworkers, involved himself and his union in local Community Chest drives, in sending "legislative representatives" from the union locals to state legislatures, and in participating in the then Republican administration. His cross-country tour of steel mills with the president of U.S. Steel eventually led to charges that he was living too close to management. This was not unusual: earlier leaders (in this and other unions) were criticized as "class collaborators." See Lloyd Ulman, *The Government of The Steel Workers Union*, (New York: Wiley, 1962), pp. 149–50.

    It is also interesting to note what McDonald's biographers said of him:

    > . . . he is equally at home and welcomed in the millionaire clubs like Pittsburgh's austere Duquesne Club, as well as in union halls. Some snipers object to his crossing lines, but it has helped promote understanding in the big picture of labor management relations.

    See George Kelly and Edwin Beachler, *Man of Steel: The Story of David J. McDonald* (New York: North American Book Company, 1954).
49. Compare Ross, *Trade Union Wage Policy*, chap. 4, with George P. Schultz and Charles A. Myers, "Union Wage Decisions and Employment" *American Economic Review*, 40 (June 1950): 363–380.

7. PRICE & NONPRICE RATIONING OF UNION MEMBERSHIPS

1. This expression is taken from Becker, "Union Restrictions on Entry," where b is the pecuniary income differential arising from union membership, y is the annual pecuniary income expected by a new member, n is the number of years an *applicant* expects rents to continue, and r is the discount rate. Note that b and y are in pecuniary terms and thus ignore the value of nonpecuniary wealth, if any, that the union may produce. If we allow for nonpecuniary sources of rent in the calculation of F, so that F corresponds to ϱ_T in (1), no doubt y will be larger, say y'. The ration b, however, will be larger—say b'—only if nonpecuniary *alternative* income is a smaller fraction of pecuniary income than is its union counterpart. There is no reason to expect b' to be smaller than b in a proprietary union.
2. See Joan Robinson, *The Economics of Imperfect Competition* (London: MacMillan, 1933) for discussion of these pricing schemes.
3. In New York City, a special capital market for loans to purchase taxi medallions exists.
4. See Bernam, *Worker Owned Plywood Companies*, p. 130.
5. Interest rate differentials may arise where individual members find access to capital markets relatively more costly than organizations.
6. This is the money equivalent of the individual's expected utility derived from the purchase of a union card.
7. Unlike the analysis found in Powel, "Theory of Union Behavior," chap. 2, pp. 29–31, this argument does not require *differences* in the marginal utility of income

between "the union" and would-be applicants. At the margin, the size of the in-cumbent membership provides a more efficient risk bearing alternative to any given would-be member than does self-insurance, provided that the assumption in footnote 5 obtains.

8. This argument is consequently similar to the "franchise" argument suggested by Martin L. Burstein in "The Economics of Tie-in Sales," *Review of Economics and Statistics*, 42 (February 1960): 68–73, as one of a number of explanations for *full line forcing* and tie-in sales in product markets. In fact, where the union is unsuc-cessful in bargaining for dues checkoffs, and where monitoring member incomes to accurately assess income contingent periodic payments is costly, it may be more economical to tie income contingent *services* such as life insurance and medical in-surance to membership, and charge prices above marginal cost. This suggests that the incidence of dues checkoffs should be inversely related to the incidence of in-come contingent services provided by unions to their membership.

9. Berman, *Worker Owned Plywood Companies*, p. 130.

10. Where an ostensible policy of dues uniformity obtains, rebates may be employed. For over a decade, Houston longshore unions operated closed shop hiring halls. Whenever demands exceeded union membership, nonmembers were permitted to work at the union wage rate. *All* workers were tithed five percent of their gross earnings for using the halls, *but the membership was rebated its contribution*. In this way the union extracted rents from nonincumbents. See Donald L. Martin, "Claims to Work Opportunity" (Ph.D. dissertation, UCLA, 1969), pp. 49–50, also National Labor Relations Board, *Decisions and Orders of the N.S.R.B.*, 121 N.S.R.B., pp. 389–407.

Rent extraction through rebates or kickbacks is not limited to union-nonunion members, or incumbents vs. new members. Prior to BiState regulations, rents created by union efforts on the New York waterfront were notoriously extracted from union and nonunion workers alike by kickbacks to hiring foremen employed by the union leadership. See Martin, "Claims to Work Opportunity", pp. 26–31; Weinstein, "Racketeering and Labor." Managerial discretion in unions is dis-cussed in chapt. 6.

11. See Powel, *Theory of Union Behavior* pp. 47–49. Two-part tariffs (initiation fees and periodic payments) and wage and dues differentials between incumbents and newcomers are arrangements consistent with the conventional price discrimination literature. The interpretation given them in this analysis, however, is different. Pricing regimes of the sort discussed above are a function of risk spreading eco-nomies or capital market disparities. Their existence is consistent with identical de-mand elasticities for union membership for incumbents and newcomers.

12. This assumes that the elasticity of substitution between higher paid workers and capital does not differ significantly from the elasticity of substitution between lower paid workers and capital. If the latter elasticity were *greater* than the former elasticity, rent-transfering wage differentials would not provide incentives for firms to substitute toward lower paid workers. This latter hypothesis was used by Rosen ("Unionism and Occupational Wage Structure") to model a rent-maximizing union that practiced wage discrimination among its members. His evidence largely rejected that model and its assumptions requiring differences in the elasticity of substitution for capital.

13. James Heckman and George Neumann found that the return to education, a proxy for skill, was relatively lower in union jobs than in nonunion jobs. This means that, holding years of schooling constant, union contracts transfer rents from higher skilled to lower skilled workers. If tenure in membership is correlated with skill,

this means that incumbents transfer some rent to newcomers through a narrowing of wage differentials. This result is inconsistent with the proprietary model. See James J. Heckman and George A. Neumann, "Union Wage Differentials and the Decision to Join Unions," University of Chicago (unpublished).

14. See Steven N. S. Cheung, "The Structure of a Contract and the Theory of a Nonexclusive Resource," *Journal of Law and Economics,* 13 (April 1970); and Powel, *Theory of Union Behavior.*

15. Monitoring costs lend determinancy to the problem of the optimal two-part tariff. Powell (*Theory of Union Behavior*) and Cheung ("Structure and Theory").

16. Without price discrimination in memberships, it would be virtually impossible to maintain price discrimination among employers, as members in lower-rent employment would flow to higher-rent employments, dissipating differentials in their wake.

17. But of course this policy runs the risk that firms will want to substitute the less expensive new worker for the more expensive new worker and threaten the solidarity of the union, as previously discussed.

18. Leon Applebaum, "Dues and Fees Structure of Local Unions," *Monthly Labor Review,* vol. 89, no. 11 (November 1966), pp. 1236–1240. These unions charged a uniform fee to all members. Another sample of 722 locals posted minimum and maximum fee schedules. Roughly, 34 percent of this number posted fees in excess of $50.

19. See Lewis, *Unionism and Relative Wages in the United States: An Empirical Inquiry* (Chicago: University of Chicago Press, 1963), chap. 6.

20. An absolute wage differential of $1,000 per year for a period of four years, based on average nonunion income of $10,000 per year, yields a present value of $9,780 at a 10 percent rate of discount.

21. Applebaum, "Dues and Fees."

22. The market in taxi medallions is by no means unique. Liquor licenses, broadcasting licenses and airline routes generate monopoly rents for their owners and have been observed to command their capitalized values with exchange.

23. See Becker, "Union Restrictions on Entry," p. 221.

24. The Taft-Hartley Act (1974) and the Landrum Griffin Act (1959).

25. Legislation prohibiting "excessive" fees was passed in response to reports and evidence that "corrupt" unions were "bleeding" their members by charging exorbitant fees. Although this may only have been rent extraction of the kind discussed above, the legislative response was to corruption in unions and *not* to a revelation of the monopoly value of a union card.

26. To my knowledge, Becker, "Union Restrictions on Entry," was the first to point this out. He believes that this argument is sufficient to dismiss *imperfect capital markets* as an explanation of "low" initiation prices. See also Powel, *Theory of Union Behavior.*

27. Under nonproprietary assumptions, incumbents will also seek to retard increases in dues and assessments levied on them, behaving as if their rate of time discount were higher than the rate of return to the union for further investments in rent-enhancing activities. It may be objected that rent-enhancing investment by the collective raises the value of monopoly rents to *all* incumbents, and therefore freerider resistance to dues increases will also be present under proprietary unionism. However, the resistance will be even greater if future rents cannot be capitalized into present transfer prices, as is the case in the nonproprietary union.

Similarly, nonproprietary unions should pay less attention to revenue obtainable from the sale of *work permits* to temporary, nonunion workers beyond the point where such funds no longer provide a substitute for contributions to union treasuries by incumbents. This is, perhaps, why many unions fail to price *work permits* to clear the market when they are issued. See Herbert Lahne, "The Union Work Permit," *Political Science Quarterly*, September 1951, pp. 350-80.

28. Rosen, "Unionism and Occupational Wage Structure;" Richard B. Freeman, "Unionism and the Distribution of Labor Incomes," Harvard University and National Bureau of Economic Research (1977); Heckman and Neumann, "Union Wage Differentials."

29. See J. L. Medoff, "Layoffs and Alternatives Under Trade Unionism," p. 393.

30. This is consistent with H. Gregg Lewis's observation that the greatest increases in union/nonunion wage differentials and therefore in union rents have occurred during periods of declining labor demands. That is, wage rigidity and differential layoff practices favoring incumbents have transfered rents from junior to senior members. See Lewis, *Unionism and Relative Wages*, chap. 6.

31. Institutional labor economists, beginning with the Webbs, reported the importance and significance of wage uniformity. See Sidney Webb and Beatrice Webb, *Industrial Democracy* (Longmans, Green and Co., 1902).

32. Rosen, "Unionism and Occupational Wage Structure."

33. Freeman, "Unionism and Skill Differentials."

34. However, as discussed above, the marginal returns to larger memberships can turn negative. For example, minority groups form Globe election units and play off incumbent managers against rival affiliations.

35. Finding initiation fees and dues relatively low, Taft, *Structure and Government of Labor Unions*, concludes that the demand elasticity of membership in unions must be relatively high, suggesting that otherwise unions would have raised fees and dues to much higher levels. But it takes more than just an examination of the absolute values of fees and dues to draw conclusions concerning elasticity. In a recent paper on the demand for memberships, Pencavel—using data from British unions—found that dues elasticity has been quite low, and concluded that "the [evidence] gives empirical support to those union leaders who have called for higher union dues to bolster impecunious union finances." See John Pencavel, "The Demand for Union Services: An Exercise," *Industrial and Labor Relations Review,* 24 (January 1971): 180-90.

36. See Taft, *Structure and Government of Labor Unions,* chap. 3.

37. Benefit programs have been known to include air travel and group tours, retirement homes, buying programs, vitamin and drug discount programs, and group legal services.

38. The savings in postage alone through the union's nonprofit mailing permit may create a major economy for the organization.

39. This proposition is not affected by the introduction of positive transaction costs associated with side payments, where such costs are a rising function of the size of membership.

40. There is much to be cautious about in using wage differentials as a measure of monopoly power. See Becker, "Union Restrictions on Entry"; Rice, "Skill, Earnings, and Growth"; and Kochin, "Social Cost."

41. See Herbert Hill, "Discrimination and Trade Unions, Comment" in *Discrimination in Labor Markets*, ed. Orley Ashenfelter and Albert Rees (Princeton, N.J.: Princeton University Press, 1973), pp. 113-24.

42. Although union treasuries may be increased by pricing new memberships to reflect potential monopoly rents, irrespective of ownership characteristics, a member of a nonproprietary union has a more tenuous personal claim on such funds than a member of a proprietary union.

43. The referral/nonreferral classification is actually preferred by Orley Ashenfelter, "Discrimination and Trade Unions" in *Discrimination in Labor Markets*, ed. Orley Ashenfelter and Albert Rees (Princeton, N.J.: Princeton University Press, 1973), p. 97, fn 13.

44. This differs from Ashenfelter's view that "craft unions tend to have greater control of the supply of labor and of the hiring process than do industrial unions, and *this also will tend to make them more discriminatory*." (Italics supplied.) Under nonproprietary conditions, economic theory does not unambiguously predict that craft unions will be more discriminatory than industrial unions. Rather, it predicts that discrimination will take different forms between the two union types.

References

Alchian, Armen A., "The Basis of Some Recent Advances in the Theory of Management of the Firm," *Journal of Industrial Economics* 14 (November 1965): 30-41.

———. "Corporate Management and Property Rights" in *Economic Policy and the Regulation of Corporate Securities*. Washington, D.C.: American Enterprise Institute, 1969.

Alchian, Armen A., and Demsetz, Harold. "Production Information Costs and Economic Organization." *American Economic Review* 62 (December 1972): 777-95.

Ashenfelter, Orley. "Discrimination and Trade Unions." In *Discrimination in Labor Markets*. Ed. Orley Ashenfelter and Albert Rees. Princeton, N.J.: Princeton University Press, 1973.

Ashenfelter, Orley, and Johnson, George. "Bargaining Theory, Trade Unions and Industrial Strike Activity." *American Economic Review* 59 (March 1969): 35-49.

Ashenfelter, Orley; Johnson, George; and Pencavel, John. "Trade Unions and the rate of Change of Money Wages in United States Manufacturing Industry." *Review of Economic Studies*, 1971.

Applebaum, Leon. "Dues and Fees Structure of Local Unions," *Monthly Labor Review* 89, no. 11 (November 1966): 1236-40.

Atherton, Wallace. *Theory of Union Bargaining Goals*. Princeton, N.J.: Princeton University Press, 1973.

Becker, Gary S. *The Economics of Discrimination*. Chicago: University of Chicago Press, 1957.

———. "Union Restrictions on Entry," in *The Public Stake in Union Power*. Phillip D. Bradley, Ed. Charlottesville, Va.: University of Virginia Press, 1959.

Berkowitz, Monroe. "The Economics of Trade Union Organization and Administration." *Industrial and Labor Relations Review* 7 (July 1954): 575-92.

Berle, Adolph and Means, Gardner. *The Modern Corporation and Private Property*. New York: MacMillan, 1932.

Bird, Monroe and Robinson, James. "The Effectiveness of the Union Label and Buy Union Campaigns," *Industrial and Labor Relations Review* 25 (July 1972): 512-23.

Burstein, Martin L., "The Economics of Tie-in Sales." *Review of Economics and Statistics* 42 (February 1960): 68-73.

147

Cartter, Alan. *Theory of Wages and Employment*. Homewood, Ill.: 1959. R.D. Irwin.

Chapin, Gene L. "The Union as an Economic Enterprise: An Exploratory Essay." Ohio University Department of Economics, 1971 (unpublished).

Cheung, Steven N.S. "The Structure of a Contract and the Theory of a Nonexclusive Resource." *Journal of Law and Economics* 13 (April 1970): 49-70.

Clarkson, Kenneth W. "Organization Constraints and Models of Managerial Behavior." In *The Economics of Nonproprietary Institutions*, Ed. Kenneth W. Clarkson and Donald L. Martin. Greenwich, Conn.: J.A.I. Press, 1980.

———. "Some Implications of Property Rights in Hospital Management," *Journal of Law and Economics* 15 (October 1972): 373-84.

Cohen, M. "The Determinants of the Relative Supply and Demand for Unskilled Workers." Ph.D. dissertation, Massachusetts Institute of Technology, 1967.

Cole, David L. "Interrelationships in the Settlement of Jurisdictional Disputes." *Labor Law Journal* 10 (July 1959): 459-60.

De Alessi, Louis. "An Economic Analysis of Government Ownership and Regulation: Theory and Evidence from the Electric Power Industry." *Public Choice* 14 (Fall 1974): 1-42.

———. Louis. "The Economics of Property Rights: A Review of the Evidence." Working Paper 78-2, Law and Economics Center, University of Miami, 1978.

Demsetz, Harold. "Some Aspects of Property Rights." *Journal of Law and Economics,* 9 (October 1966): 61-70.

———. "Toward a Theory of Property Rights." *American Economic Review* 57 (May 1967): 61-70.

Directory of National Unions and Employee Associations, 1975, Bureau of Labor Statistics Bulletin, 1937.

Dunlop, John. *Wage Determination Under Trade Unionism*. New York: Macmillan, 1944.

Ehrenberg, Ronald and Goldberg, Steven. "Officer Performance and Compensation in Local Building Trade Unions." *Industrial and Labor Relations Review* 30, no. 3 (January 1977): 188-96.

Estey, Marten, *The Unions: Structure, Development, and Management* (New York: Harcourt, Brace & World), 1967.

Estey, Marten; Taft, Philip; and Wagner, Martin. *Regulating Union Government*. New York: Harper and Row, 1964.

Fellner, William. *Competition Among the Few*. New York: A.A. Knopf, 1949.

Feinberg, Robert M. "Utility Maximization vs. Profit Maximization." *Southern Economic Journal* 42 (July 1975): 130-32.

Frech III, H.E. "Ted". "The Property Rights Theory of the Firm: Empirical Results from a Natural Experiment." Working Paper #28, Department of Economics, University of California at Santa Barbara, December 1974.

Freeman, Richard B. "Unionism and the Distribution of Labor Incomes." Harvard University and National Bureau of Economic Research, 1977 (unpublished).

Goldner, W. "Labor Market Factors and Skill Differentials in Wage Rates." Industrial Relations Research Association, Proceedings of the Tenth Annual Meeting, 1958.

Goldstein, G.S. and Pauly, M.V. "Group Health Insurance as a Local Public

Good." In *The Role of Health Insurance in the Health Services Sector*, Ed. Richard Rosett. New York: National Bureau of Economic Research, 1976, chap. 3.

Gorman, Robert A. *Labor Law, Unionization and Collective Bargaining*. St. Paul: West Publishing Co., 1976.

Greene, Mark. *The Role of Employee Benefit Structures in Manufacturing Industry*. University of Oregon, 1964.

Grodin, Joseph R., *Union Government and the Law*, Institute of Industrial Relations, University of California at Los Angeles, 1961.

Hill, Herbert. "Discrimination and Trade Unions, Comment." In *Discrimination in Labor Markets*, Ed. Orley Ashenfelter and Albert Rees. Princeton, N.J.: Princeton University Press, 1973.

Hilton, George. "The Theory of Tax Incidence Applied to the Gains of Labor Unions." In *The Allocation of Economic Resources*, ed. M. Abromovitz and others, Stanford, Ca.: Stanford University Press, 1959.

Hutchinson, John R. "The Anatomy of Corruption in Trade Unions." *Industrial Relations* 8, no. 2 (1969): 135-50.

Jensen, Michael, and Meckling, William. "Theory of the Firm: Managerial Behavior, Agency Costs, and Ownership Structure." *Journal of Financial Economics* (October 1976): 305-60.

Johnson, George E. "Economic Analysis of Trade Unionism." *American Economic Review* 67 (May 1975): 23-28.

Kelly, George and Beachler, Edwin. *Man of Steel: The Story of David J. McDonald*. New York: North American Book Company, 1954.

Kerr, Clark. "Economic Analysis and the Study of Industrial Relations." Reprint. Berkeley and Los Angeles University of California Press, 1948.

Kochin, Levis A. "The Social Cost of Union Monopoly." University of Washington Department of Economics, (unpublished), 1977.

Krislov, Joseph. "Raiding Among the Legitimate Unions." *Industrial and Labor Relations Review*, 8, no. 1 (October 1954): 19-29.

———. "The Extent of Trends of Raiding Among American Unions." *Quarterly Journal of Economics* 69 (February 1955): 152.

Lahne, Herbert. "The Union Work Permit." *Political Science Quarterly* (September 1951), pp. 350-80.

Larrowe, Charles P. *Shape-up and Hiring Hall*. Berkeley and Los Angeles: University of California Press, 1955.

Lester, Richard A. "Shortcomings of Marginal Analaysis for Wage-Employment Problems." *American Economic Review* 36 (March 1946): 63-82.

———. "Benefits as a Preferred Form of Compensation." *Southern Economic Journal*, 33, 4 (April 1967): 488-95.

Lewis, H. Gregg, "Competitive and Monopoly Unionism." In *The Public Stake in Union Power*, ed. Philip D. Bradley, Charlottesville, Va.: University Press of Virginia, 1959.

———. *Unionism and Relative Wages in the United States: An Empirical Inquiry*. Chicago: University of Chicago Press, 1963.

Lindblom, Charles. *Unions and Capitalism*. New Haven, Ct.: Yale University Press, 1949.

Lipset, Seymour; Trow, Martin; and Coleman, James. *Union Democracy: The In-*

ternal Politics of the International Typographical Union. Glencoe, Ill.: Free Press, 1956.

Machlup, Fritz. "Marginal Analysis and Empirical Research." *American Economic Review* 36 (March 1946): 519-54.

Mendelson, A.I. "Fringe Benefits Today and Tomorrow." *Labor Law Journal*, June 1956, pp. 325-28 and pp. 379-84.

Martin, Donald L. "Job Property Rights and Job Defections." *Journal of Law and Economics* 15 (October 1972): 385-410.

————. "Some Economics of Job Property Rights in the Longshore Industry." Journal of Economics and Business, Winter 1973, pp. 93-100.

————. "Unions as Nonproprietary Institutions." In *The Economics of Nonproprietary Institutions*, ed. Kenneth W. Clarkson and Donald L. Martin. Greenwich, Conn.: J.A.I. Press, 1980.

Mason, Edward. "Labor Monopoly and All That." *Industrial Relations Research Association Proceedings*. December 1955, pp. 188-213.

Mitchell, Daniel, J.B. "Union Wage Policies: The Ross-Dunlop Debate Reopened." *Industrial Relations* 11 (1972): 46-61.

————. "Labor and the Tariff Question." *Industrial Relations* 9 (May 1970): 268-276.

Moore, John. "Uncertainty and Sticky-Downward But Upward-Mobile Wages." *Economic Inquiry* 13, 4 (December 1975): 559-64.

National Industrial Conference Board. *Handbook of Union Government Structure and Procedures*. Studies in Personnel Policy, No. 150, (no date).

Neumann, George and Heckman, James. "Union Wage Differentials and the Decision to Join Unions." Chicago: University of Chicago (unpublished), 1977.

Nichols, Alfred. "Stock Versus Mutual Savings and Loan Associations. Some Evidence of Differences in Behavior." *American Economic Review* 57 (May 1967): 337-346.

Olson, E. O. Jr., "Profit Maximization Versus Utility Maximization: A Correction." *Southern Economic Journal,* 43, 3 (January 1977): 1390-93.

Olson, Mancur. *The Logic of Collective Action*. Cambridge, Mass.: Harvard University Press, 1965.

Pen, Jan. *Journal of Economic Literature,* 12, 2 (June 1974) 536-37.

Pencavel, John. "The Demand for Union Services: An Exercise." *Industrial and Labor Relations Review* 24 (January 1971): 180-90.

Perlman, Selig, *A Theory of the Labor Movement*. 1928. Reissued New York: Augustus M. Kelley, 1949.

Petshek, Kirk R. "The Tie Between Wages and Employment." *Industrial and Labor Relations Review* 4 (November 1950): 94-99.

Powel, John. *A Theory of Union Behavior Applied to the Medical Profession*. Ph.D. dissertation, University of Washington, 1973.

Reder, Melvin. "Job Scarcity and the Nature of Union Power," *Industrial and Labor Relations Review* 13 (April 1960): 349-62.

————. "The Theory of Union Wage Policy." *Review of Economics and Statistics* 34 (February 1952): 34-45.

Rees, Albert. *The Economics of Trade Unions*. Chicago: University of Chicago Press, 1962.

Rice, Robert. "Skill, Earnings and the Growth of Wage Supplements." *American Economic Review* 56 (May 1966): 583–93.

Rosen, Sherwin. "Unionism and Occupational Wage Structure in the United States." *International Economic Review* 11 (June 1970): 269–86.

Ross, Arthur. *Trade Union Wage Policy*. Berkeley and Los Angeles: University of California Press, 1956.

Rottenberg, Simon. "Property in Work." *Industrial and Labor Relations Review*, 15 (October 1962): 402–409.

Sales, Leonard R., and Strauss, George. *The Local Union*. New York: Harcourt, Brace, and World, 1967.

Selected Earnings and Demographic Characteristics of Union Members, 1970. Bureau of Labor Statistics Report, 417, 1972.

Simons, Henry. "Some Reflections on Syndicalism." In *Economic Policy for a Free Society*. Chicago: University of Chicago Press, 1948.

Smith, Adam. *An Inquiry Into the Causes of the Wealth of Nations* (1776). New York: Modern Library, 1937.

Solnick, Loren M., and Staller, Gerome M. "The Effect of Unionism on Employer Fringe Benefit Expenditures." Paper presented at the Labor Union Session of the Western Economic Association Meetings, June 26, 1976, San Francisco, California.

Taft, Philip. *The Structure and Government of Labor Unions*. Cambridge: Harvard University Press, 1956.

Ulman, Lloyd. *The Government of the Steel Workers Union*. New York: Wiley, 1962.

Warren-Boulton, Frederick. *Vertical Control of Markets: Business and Labor Practices*. Cambridge, Mass.: Ballinger Publishing Co., 1978.

Webb, Sidney, and Webb, Beatrice. *Industrial Democracy*. Longmans, Green & Company, 1902.

Weinstein, Paul A. "Racketeering and Labor: An Economic Analysis." *Industrial and Labor Relations Review* 14 (April 1966): 402–413.

Weiss, Lenard W. "Concentration and Labor Earnings." *American Economic Review* 56 (March 1966): 96–117.

Index

AFL-CIO (American Federation of Labor-Congress of Industrial Organizations), 40, 95, 96
Airline Pilots Association, 135 n. 19
Annable, James E., 124 n. 24
Antitrust Laws, 32-33, 127 nn. 1, 2, 131 n. 26
Ashenfelter, Orley, 16, 87, 88, 117, 118, 144 n. 44
Atherton, Wallace, 4, 8, 9, 16-23, 24, 29, 64, 67, 122 nn. 6, 8, 10, 124 nn. 25, 26, 27, 28, 32, 125 nn. 40, 45, 46, 126 n. 53
Atherton Model, 16-23, 24, 25, 26, 28, 125 nn. 37, 38, 39

Bargaining: collective, 58, 89, 99, 103-104, 125 n. 41, 127 n. 4, 133 n. 41; exclusive, 33, 48; goals of, 16-27, 66, 124 n. 32; theory of, 16-17
Becker, Gary S., 111, 112, 141 n. 1
Benefits, 78-79, 82, 116, 140 n. 34, 142 n. 8, 144 n. 37. See also Retirement
Berkowitz, Monroe, 23, 25
Berman, Katrina V., 109
Bird, Monroe, 11
Blacks. See Negroes
Bureau of Labor Statistics, 39, 111

Cartels, 11, 122 n. 7
Cartter, Alan, 21, 64, 124 n. 25, 125 n. 36
Chapin, Gene L., 122 n. 1
"Cheap labor threat," 10
Civil Rights Act, 77, 128 n. 17, 134 n. 1
Clarkson, Kenneth, 129 n. 11
Closed shop, 49-50, 129 nn. 9, 10, 132 n. 36

Coleman, James, 1
Collusion rights, 32-33
Compensating margins, 48-50
Costs, 125 n. 46; of collective bargaining, 133 n. 41; of information, 123 n. 22; of reconciling differences, 13

Department of Labor, 77
Discrimination, 37, 118-119, 140 n. 40
Domar, Evsy, 131 n. 28
"Dual unionism," 93
Dunlop, John, 1, 3, 6-9, 21, 22, 122 n. 6, 123 n. 15, 126 n. 58

Economic welfare, 11-12, 14

Farm labor, 139 n. 21
Federal Rules of Civil Procedure, 33-34
Fellner, William, 124 n. 25
Female workers, 11, 45, 117. See also Minorities
Filial preference. See Membership, transfer of
Freeman, Richard B., 115
Free-rider, 49, 50, 58, 93, 132 n. 33, 136 n. 35

Gallo Brothers, Inc., 139 n. 21
Globe election, 104, 140 n. 44, 144 n. 34

Heckman, James, 115, 142 n. 13
Hicksian composite good, 53, 55, 56, 63, 76
Hilton, George, 11
Hoffa, Jimmy, 138 n. 10

ILWU, 136 n. 28
Inflation, 68, 85, 88
Internal Revenue Service, 38

International Longshoremens' and Warehousemens' Union, 135 n. 19
International Typographical Union, 141 n. 45

Jensen, Michael, 134 n. 7
Job right, 29, 52, 73
Johnson, George E., 16, 87, 88

Kerr, Clark, 10
Kickbacks, 70, 98, 142 n. 10
Kochin, Levis A., 134 n. 11

Labor demand: decrease in, 83–84, 88; increase in, 79–83, 88
Labor Management Relations Act, 33–35, 127 n. 5
Labor Management Reporting and Disclosure Act, 34, 37, 38, 39
Landrum Griffin Act, 138 n. 12
Laws, governing trade unions, 31–39, 127 nn. 1–13, 16, 128 n. 17–24, 138 n. 12
Leadership. *See* Managers
Lester, Richard A., 10
Lewis, H. Gregg 10
Lindblom, Charles, 10
Lipset, Seymour, 1
LMRA. *See* Labor Management Relations Act
LMRDA. *See* Labor Management Reporting and Disclosure Act
Longshoremens' Union, 56, 57, 135 n. 19, 136 n. 28
Longshoring industry, 129 N. 5, 132 n. 37, 134 n. 2, 135 n. 19, 136 n. 28

McClellan hearings, 104
McDonald, David, 141 n. 48
Machlup, Fritz, 10
Management. *See* Managers
Managers: union, 90–107; closeness of to management, 141 n. 48; in competition for rents, 115–116; discretion of, 123 n. 20, 134 n. 7, 138 nn. 11, 13, 140 n. 33; leadership of, 139 nn. 26, 27, 28, 140 n. 30; monitoring performance of, 102, 137 n. 4; personal power of, 11, 13; salaries of, 98, 103, 136 n. 23, 140 nn. 30, 39
Meckling, William, 134 n. 7
Medical profession as model, 29

Medoff, J. L., 115
Membership: distribution, 39–46; dues and fees, 82, 116, 119, 142 nn. 10, 11, 143 nn. 18, 25, 26, 27, 144 nn. 35, 42; entry restriction for, 132 nn. 35, 36, 133 n. 43, 141 n. 1; function of, 123 n. 14; managers, role in, 82, 138 n. 9; price discrimination in, 111, 143 n. 16; rationing of, 108–119; rights of, 35–36, 134 n. 4; sale of, 81, 91; socioeconomic characteristics of, 44–46; transfer of, 71, 72, 73, 74, 77, 128 n. 17, 134 nn. 1, 3
Membership-employment expansion, 82–83, 135 n. 15
Minorities, 12–13, 44–45
Minors, 11
Mitchell, Daniel J. B., 11
Mitchell, John, 131 n. 26
Monopoly, 2, 9, 12, 15; of rents, 21, 22, 28, 30, 33, 50–53, 73, 118, 126 n. 60, 129 n. 12, 130 nn. 13, 16, 17, 137 n. 3; of wage rates, 11, 28, 29
Moore, John, 65–66, 83–84

National Industrial Conference Board, 136 n. 36
National Labor Relations Act, 33, 96, 127 n. 3, 139 n. 21
National Labor Relations Board, 13, 34, 97, 127 n. 4
Negroes, 37, 44. *See also* Nonwhites
Net revenue, maximization, 25, 26, 27, 28, 29; union, 23, 24
Neumann, George, 115, 142 n. 13
New Deal, 112
New York Stock Exchange, 35, 57, 72, 131 nn. 26, 27
NLRB. *See* National Labor Relations Board
Nonprice rationing, 116–119
Nonproprietary union, 71–89; managerial constraints in, 92–95, 106–107
Nonwhites, 117–119. *See also* Negroes
NRM. *See* Net revenue, maximization

Oliphant vs. Brotherhood of Local Firemen, 37
Ownership, 3, 31–46, 73–75, 86–88; characteristics of, 30; separation from control of, 123 nn. 19, 20

Pacific Maritime Association, 135 n. 19
Participation rights, 36-38
Pencavel, John, 111, 144 n. 35
Petshek, Kirk, 11
Plywood co-op, worker-owned, 35, 37, 72, 109, 131
Postage, 39, 144 n. 38
Powel, John, 2, 28, 29, 126 n. 60, 133 n. 39
Price level: effects on union bargaining goals, 66, 124 n. 33; on union wage policy, 84-89, 124 n. 34
Profit maximization, 2, 3, 9-10, 13, 25, 126 n. 47
Property, union ownership of, 35-36
Property rights, 3, 4, 5; private, 8, 9, 26, 71-75
Proprietary trade unions, 56-70

Racketeers, 134 n. 6
Raid, the, 95-97
Railway Brotherhood, 37
Railway Labor Act, 36, 37
Reder, Melvin, 9
Retirement, 132 n. 37, 135 n. 19
Rice, Robert, 129 n. 12
Robinson, James, 11
Rosen, Sherwin, 2, 115, 130 n. 17
Ross, Arthur, 1, 4, 9, 10, 11-16, 17, 23, 123 nn. 18, 21, 137 n. 2
Ross Model, 10-16

Secretary of Labor, 34, 37
Senate Select Committee on Improper Practices in Labor Management Field, 141 n. 46
Simons, Henry, 122 n. 7
Smith, Adam, 1
Solnick, Loren M., 78, 79
Staller, Gerome M., 78, 79
Strikes, 17, 18, 19, 20, 48, 50, 51, 52, 67, 86-88, 124 nn. 27, 31, 125 n. 37, 136 nn. 32, 34-36, 38, 137 n. 41

Taft, Philip, 111, 138 n. 13, 144 n. 35
Taft-Hartley Act, 37, 112, 128 n. 17, 129 nn. 8, 10

Target rate, 21
Target zone, 20-21, 124 n. 25
Tariff protection, 11
Teamsters Union, 40, 138 n. 10, 139 n. 21
Theory of Union Bargaining Goals, 16
Trade Union Wage Policy, 9, 13
Trow, Martin, 1
Trust funds, 98

Union admission policies, 36, 37; behavior, 16-27, 123 n. 22; goals, 10, 14, 125 n. 40; labeling of, 11; and shop, 49-50, 129 n. 9, 10, 132 n. 36; structure of, 39-46; survival and growth of, 11
United Automobile Workers, 40
United Farmworkers, 139 n. 21
United States Constitution, 37
United Steelworkers, 141 n. 48
Unit elasticity, definition of, 7
Utility maximization, 16-23, 24, 26, 27, 30, 53-56, 124 n. 25, 126 n. 47

Wage bill: definition of, 122 n. 3; and maximization, 3, 7-9, 21, 22; model of, 122 nn. 4, 6
Wage demands, 10, 123 n. 15; determination of, 122 n. 5; differentials in, 135 n. 21, 142 n. 13, 144 nn. 30, 40; dispersion of, 135 n. 21; elasticity of, for labor, 58-59, 132 n. 33; and membership income, 7, 12-13; and membership policy, 102-106; policy, 7, 16, 123 n. 15; rates of, 19-20, 122 n. 10, 131 n. 25
Wage-employment constraints, 17, 18, 19, 20; relationship of, 9-10, 17, 18, 19, 123 n. 18
Wage-membership policy, 102-106
Wagner Act, 132 n. 33
Wealth maximand, 2, 3, 4, 5, 6, 7, 9, 10, 11, 12, 13, 27-30, 126 n. 58
Weiss, Lenard W., 10
Work rules, 12
Worker-owned plywood co-op, 35, 57, 72, 109, 131

Compositor: Freedmen's Organization
Type: Times Roman, Compugraphic
Printer: Braun-Brumfield, Inc.
Paper: 50lb P&S Vellum

Decl 4/01110CP

MARTIN